July 21, 2017

# Let Your Dog Out!

## A Spiritual Journey

Dear Nathalie:

Thank you for your friendship.
I love that you don't fit in a box or
stay within the lines.
We are in each other's life for a
reason. Thank you for showing up.

love ya!

Namasté

# SPIRIT JORDACHE

authorHOUSE®

AuthorHouse™
1663 Liberty Drive
Bloomington, IN 47403
www.authorhouse.com
Phone: 1 (800) 839-8640

Published by AuthorHouse 07/01/15

ISBN: 978-1-5049-2043-8 (sc)
ISBN: 978-1-5049-2042-1 (hc)
ISBN: 978-1-5049-2055-1 (e)

Library of Congress Control Number: 2015910677

# CONTENTS

# AKNOWLEDGMENTS

I would like to thank my wife Lilou Jordache for her patience and encouragement during the second five years of my journey. It has been a wonderful trip being married to you. I Love you.

I would like to thank all the people that contributed to my spiritual awakening; Tina for introducing me to the world of motivators and great thinkers. You got me going, and I took off from there. I love your energy and your awesome laugh.

Thank you Dani for introducing me to religion, reading scripture with you got my heart and mind in the spiritual mode, and my curiosity awakened about Jesus and his teachings. No matter what path we choose, we are all headed into the same direction. Blessings.

Thank you Tash. You gave me shelter when I needed it most.

Thank you Olivia, for the time we spent together. Though it seemed we were dysfunctional in many ways, all that drama that we had was absolutely necessary in order to put us where we are today. We had great times too and I will always cherished them.

Thank you to Pepe and Claudia, without you I would have never met my wife.

Finally I would like to express my total gratitude to those beautiful creatures that have accompanied me through out this journey. "Morris", "Zorro", "Chubaka", "Trece", "Lobo" and "Orly"; you have been the ultimate spiritual teachers. Since you cannot read these words, I'll make sure an extra treat, or two, make their way out to you. Namaste.

# INTRODUCTION

The inspiration for this book started one day, ten years ago, when I was reading one of many inspirational books I had decided to read in an attempt to create a change within me. As I started to read and get into the messages from the author, I realized, suddenly, that my best teachers were right in front of me.....................................my dogs!

Yes my dogs, and they had many, many answers about life. However, because I had been living in what I call "Limbo," or you may call "Hell," or "Ego," I had not been paying attention to their daily teachings. I was living a lie, and I was so immersed in my own head to see all their messages. The purpose here is to show you that a person as deep in Limbo as I was, can change and show you that a "regular" person can awaken, and it is not only the Spiritual leaders who can. We all can Let Our Dog Out!!

This book will show you how, by simple observation of your beloved pets, or in fact any animal; you can acquire the most fundamental and important spiritual state of mind you could ever be: BE HERE AND NOW.

I will show you how your Limbo or voice in the head, also known as your ego; it is not who you really are and how to go about observing that voice and tell it to be silent. You will accompany me through my journey and understand how deeply controlled, by our limbo, most of us are, and how to detach from it. Then learn to live from your dog perspective. Here and now.

This book will show you how all paths of our spiritual journeys are all correct, yet different. You will see how our journey is as individual and unique as our fingerprints. And our teachers are also different for each student who is ready. You will learn to simplify your lessons and your learning, by understanding that the lessons of Jesus, Buddha, Dalai Lama or Eckhart Tolle; are within the teachings of your dogs, all you have to do is decode them.

As you progress through this book, you will learn to see all animals, events and situations as another opportunity to learn, and reach enlightenment. You will understand that frustrations, set backs and transformation are all necessary as a path from suffering to enlightenment.

However, let me back up a little. Let me introduce you to my teachers. "Morris", a 11-year-old Puggle. He is almost 45 pounds of pure muscle and an insatiable need to chew anything within his reach, especially if it is a "NO-NO". Those of you that know Puggles know that their average weight is 20-25 pounds, so "Morris" probably came from very big and athletic parents. "Trece"(Thirteen in Spanish), my favorite number and the queen of the house. She is a Yorkie- Pekinese mix. 9 years old and a 10-pound ball of hair and fat that is also the ruler of the house. "Chubaka" or "Chubis", a 6-pound Yorkie-Brussels Griffon-Cairn Terrier mix. He would be like the Brad Pitt of dogs. Everybody thinks he is gorgeous. All he wanted was to be loved and give love. Rest in Peace. "Lobo", a 8 year old, 15-pound mutt, son of "Trece" and "Chubis", so you figure out all the breeds in him. An escape artist by nature, and the one that brings his true self to light at every minute of the day. "Zorro",a 12 years old, 30-pound Pug-Yorkie mix, if you can even imagine such a combination. Funny body, overweight, with skinny legs!

You should know that two of my teachers, are not living with me. "Chubis" (before he died) and "Zorro" live with my ex-girlfriend and also a teacher in many ways, Olivia. She was my last relationship that ended because of my thick and dark "Limbo," but pushed me to try to understand myself and become aware of my hell, through the eyes of my teachers.

As you read this book, you may ask yourself, where do you find teachers like mine? You can go to any shelter and rescue one, buy a fancy pure breed one, observe your friend's teacher(s), go to the dog park, the farm, watch National Geographic Wild. There you will find your lessons in love, lessons in kindness, lessons in Heaven, and lessons in awareness and energy.

Nothing that I have written is earth shattering, or a new discovery. But then again, neither are all the self-help, spiritual books. Jesus, Buddha, and many other great minds had already given the message to find Heaven on Earth. My first great minds are my dogs. So join me in the journey to find myself, and to "Let My Dog Out!" And hopefully it will give you insights into how to let yours out, too. In conclusion, my pets wrote this book, I just arranged the messages the best I could... Namaste.

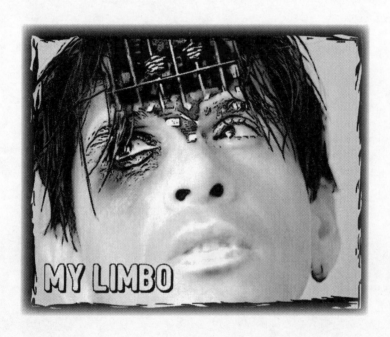

# CHAPTER 1

## My Limbo

Main Entry: **lim·bo** Pronunciation: \'lim-(ˌ)bō\

Function: *noun* Inflected Form(s): *plural* **limbos**

Etymology: Middle English, from Medieval Latin, abl. of *limbus* limbo, from Latin, border Date: 14th century

*often capitalized:* an abode of souls that are according to Roman Catholic theology barred from heaven because of not having received Christian baptism, a place or state of restraint or confinement **b:** a place or state of neglect or oblivion <proposals kept in limbo> **c:** an intermediate or transitional place or state **d:** a state of uncertainty

What you are about to read is the story of my Limbo, not with the purpose of getting pity or admiration but to show you that you can insert your story, your Limbo, into this book, and you can too, find the way out into the light. My Limbo started probably since I was a little child. I was born late July in1963, in a small city in central Mexico, called Guanajuato. Mauricio, was the name given by my parents, was born to a family comprised of my father Agustin, who is no longer physically present in this Earth, but for sure in spirit and energy.

My mother Maria, who was as close to a Saint as I have ever encountered, who chose a path of suffering as her comfort zone, and therefore, she had her own Limbo. She moved into the world of energy in May of 2013. My older brother, who hopefully someday will find peace and harmony as he goes through this life with his own Limbo to conquer, just like the rest of us. After me came another brother eight years younger, who tries in his own way to have a "light Limbo," and my baby brother,fourteen years younger who has learned so much from reading, but who hasn't applied the golden rule, "Take care of yourself first, before you can help anybody else." When we were young, my father severely physically and mentally abused me. My dad's Limbo was so dense that he had no way of noticing what was happening to him. He was brutally abused as a child, so he carried inside all this anger, which he eventually let out, on my my mother and myself.

Back when this was happening to me, I made a choice. A poor choice. I accepted my parent's stories as "normal," and Bam! My Limbo was created. I created MY story based on the examples given to me by parents, brothers, and friends. I was too young to realize that better ways existed. Abuse, verbal and physical were the norm of the house. I either was to accept it or reject it. I created my Limbo by rejecting abuse as the norm for my life, but I acquired self-help mechanisms, that were just as dysfunctional as the abuse itself. I became shy, withdrawn, a loner and had zero self-esteem.

As the years went by I identified myself with the roles I had created. I was comfortable saying, "I'm shy," and therefore, I acted the role. "Nobody loves me," and again, I would play the role of an unloved one. I could have won an academy award. Every role that I played was "on the money," with tears, and dramatic displays that would put to shame any actor trying to play such roles. I was an artist.... I still think we are all artists, but as you will see later, not the same way as I thought back then. I was so sure I "knew" who I was, that, if somebody disagreed, I had examples and long explanations on why I was truly who I believe to be and everyone else was wrong.

I always loved the arts, and I was very good at it. I developed my talents as dancer, painter, and actor. I was very successful at it, and it came as an easy hobby. I was so lost in my Limbo that even then I failed to recognize that through the arts, you can develop a silent mind. I had glimpses of Heaven, but I did not see it. I did not learn it, and of course I never applied it. When I was immersed in the Arts, I truly was free from Ego. There was no shyness, no lack of self-esteem, no Limbo. If I weren't so lost, I could have figured out that the Arts or Sports could have been a way out of my roles, but I was so stubborn, and I even found a way to explain it by saying, "That's just a way of me getting out of my shell for a few minutes," the message was right there...get out of the shell!

I'm sure that whoever you are, you had moments of "art," moments when you were present on your act, in bliss, so "in the zone," that when you went back to your Limbo, it all seemed like a dream. A beautiful dream. And you hope that another moment like that will come, and you wonder when? When, in reality, we create those moments whenever we choose to, and eventually we can make it our normal state. However, we don't know that, so we keep wishing upon a star, until the next moment "comes."

We all had glimpses into the ego-less mind at one time or another. "Solutions for Life," were sent to you by the universe, by God, by energy (what do you want to call it?). Same happened to me while playing sports, not as pure or as often as in the Arts, but nevertheless, those moments came. You see, I was so passionate while playing Fut-Bol (Soccer !!! Ok!!) and Boxing, so at times I would let my mind take over and not my body, naturally I would take everything personal. Next thing I knew I was so angry that I could not perform at my best. But then I would also have those times when everything was in alignment. Pure perfection, nobody could take me out of the Zone.

I was beyond average in Arts and Sports and if I would have pursued it seriously, probably I would have been professional, but, again, I let my Limbo convince me that I was not good enough to make a living at it. I made every excuse in the book to say that I was worthless, and I did not have the right to pursue my dreams. No way! Not me! So as you may imagine I moved on to "better" things...yeah... right! My Limbo had won...and continued to win and win and win for many years to come. Never had a dog back then, no teachers around, but then again, I would have probably dismissed them too. On the good side of things, is the fact that today; I know that I was exactly where I was supposed to be at that very moment. For I could not be where I am today if it wasn't for those moments. I told the Universe "I am not good enough," so the Universe gave me exactly what I asked for. You say you are not good enough? Granted! You have to understand that the Universe is not cruel; it only gives you what you are already. It reads your energy and matches it.

By the time the time I was 21 years old I decided to come to America (USA, I mean). And you know why I came? Because my Limbo told me to run away from my love problems. "Elena", my best friend and love, was marrying somebody else. My mind said No that's not possible! Drama!!! Tears! My mind told me "If you are not with her, you can't be happy...go! Run! Geez! If I were to be suicidal, I guess I would have done some very drastic and final actions, to a truly temporary problem. I ran away instead of trying to have a conversation with her, maybe I could have convinced her. I guess I will never know but those moments, I sure wish I would have been "in the zone."

Once in this country, I went to stay with a friend. We had kept in touch through letters for the last few years, and when she invited me to come visit her in a little town in southern Oregon. I accepted, yes I ran away from Mexico, from my girl, from life.

I was feeling so out of place living in this country. I started dating my friend, even though I did not find her to be my type. My heavy Limbo, and the culture shock and the new language were giving me headaches and ulcers. I was always mad; I would blame her, unjustly I might add, for the way she cooked, the way she dressed, or many other stupid excuses. About 6 months after my visit, and my visa about to expire, my friend offered to marry me, so I could stay....why? I don't know. We were always fighting, but I had very low self-esteem and, it was better to have drama than to be alone. So, I accepted. I was going to have somebody for me, anybody! Crazy, huh?

I had arrived during the summer of 1984, and by December I was married. To think that the night before my wedding, I didn't have the fortitude to call the ceremony off, so I got married being very angry, sad and wishing somebody could have stopped my madness. As a matter of fact, The Universe did send me a savior. My friend "Elena" called me from Mexico, the day before the wedding. I guess my mother told her about it. She asked me over the phone if I was sure what I was about to do, and of course I said I didn't. I even told her "If you tell me right now to pack my bags and go back to you, I will." Of course she could not do that. I was putting my decision in her hands; I would say that it was a very cowardly move from my part. Now I know that I could have done something on my own...stand up for myself and what I wanted, but back then I needed help.

By the time we had been married 3-4 months, I wanted out. I wanted to go back to Mexico. I told my wife my intentions, however a few days later I found out that she was pregnant! To this day, she claims that she did not get pregnant on purpose, but who cares. My sense of ethics, and having been raised Catholic made me decide that I would stay with my new family, and that it was time to grow up. "Man" was born January of 1986. I was a father, working three jobs, seven days a week, learning a new language, with a heavy Limbo, and still young enough to want to party.

By 1990, I had been working so much and fighting even more that I decided to separate. Having a son was not enough love to keep me in our house. I had no love for myself, and that was what I needed. According to the voice inside my head, I needed a woman to complete me as a man, so I went searching for the one. I found many, many women that had heavy Limbos, and we dated, had sex, and moved on...I was always feeling sorry for myself for not having "The One." I didn't even know what I was looking for! I used sex as a substitute of love, and continued with my "sorry life."

In 1990, I became a Police Officer. I read somewhere that officers usually come from very dysfunctional families. I don't know about other cops, but I sure fit such a statement. I was always the first to run towards danger. "The job" gave me all the adrenaline I could ever want. I guess it was a very good substitute of the Arts and Sports. I was always "in the zone" while working as a cop. No time to think about problems, or love, or women. I wanted to find the next "bad" guy. I became a workaholic. I loved the profession. It was like "Superman" was allowed to work 40 hours a week, and I was the super hero. The job came to me easy. I knew the law, and I excelled in my performance.

During the job, the voice in the head was quiet. I had compassion for victims, and I was fair with "perps". I was always operating in the present, but I could not stay there during off- duty hours. I would take the uniform off, and Limbo would show up again. Feeling sorry for being alone, wishing for my "savior." I felt incomplete, so my time with my son, my friends, and myself became mental-hell. Relationships came and went, but never flourished into anything serious. I am sure that some of those women were worth a whole lot more, but my Limbo did not let me see it. By 1997, even my work was controlled by Limbo. The Police department fired me for a stupid mistake and an administration wanting to set an example out of somebody. My energy matched their desires, so I was the one picked coupled with my error.

They accused me of lying, which I did, over the radio, saying that I was further from a certain location than I really was, responding to a call. By the way, this is a common procedure among cops, who routinely say they are closer or further from a call to see if another officer who is "closer," will take the call we want to avoid. Yes, I know it is wrong, but by no means it is not a reason for a dismissal, or there would be no officers on the street. It was injustice at its worst, but I had to fight back. I had to be jobless for about nine months. It was hell. The voice in the head completely took over. I remember praying to God and saying, "I am not going to hurt myself, but please God, take me out of my misery." I wanted to get back at the accusers in my case. I wished for their dismissal. I cried every time I saw a Police car drive by. I was "Super-Cop", what happened?

Eventually, in my arbitration I got my job back within the first two hours of the proceedings. The Sergeants accusing me should have been fired for lying under oath, but the whole thing was swept under the carpet. Now I hated my life all around, inside the job and off-duty. My Limbo was having a blast, crying, hating, drinking, and suffering. However, I was in a very familiar place with my buddy Limbo, and I was comfortable. If I could explain better I would say that I was in the Eye of the Storm but I knew how to live within the storms, so I was in a friendly place. Every drink, every tear, every sleepless night, every minute of self-pity was welcomed. I had become a master of suffering, and suffering was my destiny, and I was going to be perfect at it.

I think by now, as you read, some of your demons have decided to come out to play. Maybe you are recalling an incident in your life where "life was not fair". Let them! Welcome them! Watch them! Just know that they don't control you. Trust me, and stay with me, if you allow your challenges and emotions to come out but not be controlled by them and just observe them, the emotion or challenge will start to dissolve. By 1998, I decided to move to another state and recharge my career as a Police Officer. I packed my stuff, with my second wife, and my best friend Mr. Limbo. Of course, now I know that making changes in your life is never the solution, if those changes are not coupled with inner change, but I did not know that at the time, so I moved thinking that my suffering would stay in the other city. Wrong.

By 1999, I was out of another marriage, and just before my divorce, I met Olivia. For the very first time I felt like I had found "the one." I was in heaven with my perfect woman, who spoke my first language, who knew my culture, and who was very attractive. She was what I was not, funny, outgoing, and independent. We were opposites, so I figured that she could show me what I was not, and I could show her some of my good traits. Perfect fit, But my journey had a long road and my insecurities were very much present.

You got to remember that it is at least four personalities in almost any relationship of two. We bring our Limbos into our relationships. My Limbo was at full force, which manifested through jealousy, possessiveness, distrust, spying. I was trying to change the way she was, even though it was the reason I had been attracted to her. Of course, we all have a journey and I am sure when we evolve we know we did many things wrong. No fault of her, I had to change but I would not have any of it at the moment.

Nevertheless, my Limbo won. By 2004 our relationship ended temporarily. Again, I entered an old, familiar place of loneliness and suffering. Back to my comfort zone. I knew exactly what was coming, and I guess I sort of welcomed it. My ex's memory fueled and fed my Limbo, and it was off and running. Nevertheless, just before we separated, one of my teachers had arrived, "Zorro". Born May 31st, eight weeks later I headed to Los Angeles to pick him up. This bundle of joy came into our lives, and looking back, I could have learned my very first lesson, and maybe our relationship would have survived, who knows, it doesn't matter anymore. Somebody said, "It Is What It Is." So true. "Zorro" showed me free will, right off the bat. Or at least, he tried. The power to choose love over any other emotion.

Even so, we choose our suffering, our drama, our Limbo. We believe whatever the voice in the head says, and usually it is degrading and negative. We believe the lies. We even say to ourselves 'I don't have a choice. That's who I am... I can't change', but if you really had a choice, if I tell you right now that you are about to learn how to have a choice, what would you choose??? Love? Happiness? Or the lies from Limbo?

"Zorro" showed me Love. And he did it all through his free will. He was throwing all his wisdom my way. Another message was there to be discovered. "Zorro" was living the moment, not dwelling on the separation from his mother and siblings. He was not depressed. He was not acting like "poor me," "I miss them."

No, he was living the moment, living the present. He was content with licking my face, biting my shoelaces and my pants. He was showing me how the present can be Heaven. I got lost in those moments too. Limbo had no room in our games. We were in the same wave of energy. We were one.

Even so, Limbo always came back, and as soon as "Zorro" slept, my old friend would return to hunt me. My suffering of my so-called problems with Olivia would crowd my head. If I could have just remained in the present moment, as when "Zorro" was awake, I know now that I would have enjoyed my moments, and I would have been satisfied even by myself.

My first lesson to you is, STAY -STAY IN THE PRESENT, always. You will learn it; I promise. So when your Limbo comes out to play, and wants to take you to your "sad" past, or your

"stressful" future, stop it! Say something to distract it, or clap, or a quick yelp, or something...do something. Become aware; be the witness of the voice in the head. Know that it is your Limbo trying to sneak in. At the very least, change your posture. It is very hard for the Limbo to make you feel bad when your posture is that of a proud, beautiful, energetic and happy person. Try it! If you add a smile, even better. However, if the smile is hard at this stage, please change your posture. You can do that much, can't you? Of course, you can!!! Eventually, it will become a habit. Like conditioning. "If I Feel bad- I Change Posture". And remember to distract the voice in the head. Those thoughts are not you. So sing, hum, meditate, play music, dance, exercise, but do something to quiet that damn voice! You hear me? Another simple practice that you can try to make it a habit, is awareness. Through awareness, all you basically do is watch and learn. However, really watch, of course for that you need a silent mind, just as you do when you watch your best loved movie or your favorite game, or a beautiful sunset.

During those times you watch and you really pay attention to every aspect of whatever you are into. If you doubt it, just try to watch yourself when you are so much into your team's game, and you will notice that your mind was empty. Studying the plays, who were moving right, who was moving wrong, etc. or where the movie is going, who is the bad player, where is the next surprise. Yes, your mind is working, but working on the logic of it. There is no ego involved. You will notice that your ego comes into play once you lose interest because the opposite team is obviously winning or the show is not capturing your attention... at the moment you start criticizing this or that player, this or that actor, or you are concerned about your phone or what you are going to do after the show. That wouldn't be awareness.

What I am asking is for the latter. Really be into it without judgment. Just watch, look at your dog or your pet or your toddler. They are perfection when practicing the now. You see?! If you were to treat yourself like your favorite match or your favorite show, you would see unreal results. You are perfect too, but you let your mind get in the middle. Clear your mind and wonderful things will come. Start creating your life, LET YOUR DOG OUT!

Can you imagine how well it feels when you concentrate in the now? And what I mean is that it doesn't matter what is going on in your life, even if is a major illness or lack of money. It is about this very moment, repeat "I have a choice to feel good and with joy. Now." Because after all, that is all you have. Even tomorrow will happen in your NOW and yesterday was happening in your NOW. You can find something to make you feel Now, yes you can. Maybe just the simple fact that you are alive, and as long as you are alive, your purpose in life is not over. Your reaction to the Now will not only dictate a nice present, but will also snow ball into a beautiful future. I hope you will stay here with me, and Let Your Dog Out!

# CHAPTER 2

## Master Zorro

B ut let me start with the story of my first pup, "Zorro", a puppy whom I had to go pick up all the way to Los Angeles. This was my first dog ever. When I was a young boy, my family had tried to have many dogs, but all of them were given away when my mom saw no interest from us, and she was left with the job of cleaning up. I loved dogs back then, but I had no clue how to go about educating them and keeping them company. When "Zorro" came he was so grateful to get out of the cage, and ran around in circles full of gratitude, after he showed his thank yous, and he had wasted all kinds of energy running, licking, pooping, and peeing, he fell asleep. Even so, it wasn't too long before he was awake, and he was back at it. Once at my home it was a joy to watch him exploring every corner of my condo, eating even what was not edible and marking his territory. Well, life had to go on, and part of it was the fact that I had to go get the mail. Because he was just a pup, I decided to keep him inside. About five minutes later, I came back. Oh boy! Was he ever happy? Dang! I never had anyone receive me that way after being gone for 5 minutes... or any time for that matter! Did he love me so much so soon? But why not? We are born into love; we are born with love; we are open to love; we seek love; we always want to give and receive love. Most importantly, we are Love, but our mind stops us from giving it or wanting to give it or receive it. Our Limbo has always said that we have to earn it or be deserving of it. Our Limbo implies that we have to work at it, or somebody has to work at it before we, or they, can deserve it. So we waste our life justifying why we, or they deserve it or not.

However, "Zorro" was not concerned with the Limbo but being who he is. He loved me at that moment because our energies matched. On the opposite, there are dogs or people that will never match with your energy and you will not get anything but fear or rejection. Nevertheless, "Zorro" loved me at that moment, with no shame, no guilt, no regret, no hesitation. Babies do the same, have you ever seen or heard people tell others, 'You are so good with babies. You should have one of your own.' Well, I don't know if I should have one of my own or not. The fact is that your energy matches theirs, and they feel safe and comfortable with you and that is 'just fine with them'.

So maybe "Zorro's" affection was not earthly love yet, but he felt safe and comfortable being Love, with either interpretation that you want to give it, it's just fine with me. The point is that when you like somebody, and you feel comfortable with him or her, why not show it? So, next time you meet someone you like, or feel 'nice' to be with, let them know....LET YOUR DOG OUT! You have my permission to go hug your loved ones, kiss them, tell them how you feel, make them feel special...you don't have to go sniff their butts or lick it!! A good hug will do! And don't be afraid to give a perfect stranger a kind word, you probably will make their day, without knowing. Try it.

But "Zorro's" big lesson was coming and believe it or not, I was not to be the student. "Zorro" was about to teach Olivia one heck of a lesson...and it wasn't to "go potty outside"!! LOL! I will tell you my observation, based on what I saw and what I felt. Still it would not be the truth, because that's what "I" saw, my perception, my opinion, and not the real truth. She, of course, would be the perfect one to tell you her Limbo, if any. However, as I write she is somewhere living her life and with hopes that all is well, and hopefully she has found happiness.

So here it is, based on my recollection of events. Which, by the way, has a lesson in itself. Everyone sees things differently than we see them. We have "their story" and they have "their story." Neither is true unless one is enlightened. And both stories are created by our own egos based on the "convenient" story that our Limbos want to create.

In other words, our "filters" or angles that we see life are different from everyone. Not right, not wrong. It just is as it is.

Anyway, here it is. I had to go to "Protect and Serve" for four days a week, ten hours a day, plus traveling time. So needless to say, "Zorro" was home alone for half a day. I asked Olivia to check on him once in a while, at the risk of knowing that she had told me that she did not particularly liked dogs or cats, or animals in general. She told me "I'll do it for you, but if he gets close I will probably kick him." Dang! Harsh statements, but I had no choice. It was either risk his harm or his loneliness. I thought I would give it a shot with her visits and then go from there. To be honest, I have no clue how long Olivia's visits with "Zorro" were. I don't know what they did. I don't know how they interacted. I know for sure that she did not kick him, or mistreated him. However, what I saw was the birth of this incredible love and respect between two living creatures. They adored each other, and still to this day. Time was better spent with each other, and being together was the highlight of the day. I saw it. I noticed how "Zorro's" attention and energy was focused in a greater strength towards her. Don't take me wrong. "Zorro" had love for all...for me, for you, for another dog or a cat...but...She was special...and it went both ways.

In a moment of Limbo- less action, I gave "Zorro" to her. Theirs was a true love story. The kind of love that I so wanted between her and I. The love that neither of us was giving each other, but we were craving. I think back, and the lesson should have been a greater one. It should have melted into our lives, but our Limbos said 'No," and we followed the darkness one more time, instead of choosing to love each other like "Zorro" loves her and vice versa.

By September of 2004, our life as a couple had come to a standstill, but not before our second teacher came along, "Morris". I will tell you about his teachings later, but "Zorro" tried to teach us so much, and so little had been learned. Who was at fault, you may ask? We were both at fault. We didn't love ourselves enough, to love someone else. We were not capable of 'Limbo-free Love'.

The details are just another story, my story. She would have a different story of the same incidents, and both would be so different. Both stories are our stories seen from our own filters, but not the total truth, and even with two teachers right in our faces, we were so into our Limbos, that their teachings went over our heads...and our story ended. I was accusing her of cheating, though I suspect was my insecurities speaking. She was accusing me of being too jealous and possessive, which is true. We never let our dogs out; we kept them inside, buried under layers of pride, jealousy, anger, pain, lack of communication, self-pity and so much more. We were blind to the lessons and we had to move on.

"Zorro", "Morris" best friend left to go with her. "Morris" and I stayed behind. "Zorro" had left but of all the books that I read, his message was very simple "Be Happy." Yes, it is that simple. Find any reason to feel good. He was trying to show us that just the power of feeling happy and excited about every circumstance is enormous! His appearance or his size or shape is never a factor. He is happy just because he is alive. Playing and sharing his love is all he needs to do. Even in the times that he was sick, he kept sharing love and subdued happiness. Yes of course, he felt ill, but not sorry for himself.

There are enough things out there that can make us happy. But we ignore the little things in life, like a flower, a likeable gesture, a beautiful person, and a nice and fresh glass of water, the sun coming up, and a nice smile. If you can focus into just getting happy and ignore your "bad" situation and concentrate in being joyful, then the energy around you will snow ball into better things. However, you have to have faith, in other words, you have to believe that something is true regardless whether you can touch it or see it now. Get blind faith into being happy. Change your mind and the things around you will change.

If "Zorro" or my other masters can have fun with a rag doll or a shoe, so can you. Be happy, be happy, and be happy. Make it your target. I promise your life will change without a doubt. Your main priority has to be feeling good no matter what. There is no circumstance under which you cannot be happy or feel good....none! LET YOUR DOG OUT!

Today "Zorro" is around 11 years old, diabetic and blind, and full of Love and licks for you. He does not have time to feel sorry for himself, and his lack of sight is not a deterrent to live a full and joyful life. Many humans with less handicaps than "Zorro", would just throw in the towel and give up on life, but not a dog. And their lack of thinking mind, in this and in all other cases, makes them superior in their capacity to adapt to adversities. They just get up and go on. God Bless you "Zorrito" for your final message before you moved away: "Our purpose in life is to live in simplicity. There is no need to judge and quantify your possessions or situations. Just be here, Now. Eventually, you will become the user of your human mind, rather than the mind using you. Then you will understand that contentment in any situation is true bliss, because whatever life throws at you; you will accept and also detach from outcome; and from that detachment and acceptance, comes action... enlightened action...dog action.

# CHAPTER 3

## Master Morris

M aster "Morris" got his name from the term of endearment that my Mom used to call me. That has been my nickname, used by my family ever since I can remember. For starters, I was either not very original naming him, or it was my Limbo trying to create an alter ego. I suspect that it was my ego creating the "other" "Morris". Somebody I could not be. A perfect, beautiful creature, or maybe what I was refusing to be.

He was born July 17th, 2004, and about eight weeks after he was born, he was shipped from Michigan. I chose him because in the pictures that they sent me, he looked very wrinkly and chubby and with big feet. He is a Puggle, a mix of a male Pug and a female Beagle. By the time "Morris" arrived, Olivia had totally changed her mind about dogs. From being a dog hater, she quickly turned into a dog lover. However, she did not approve much that I had ordered another pup. However, "Zorro" and "Morris" did not care what we thought. They smelled each others butts. They tried to establish who was boss (which to this day I have no clue who won...), they played, fought a little, but mostly they loved and loved, and loved us.

However, Oli and I were not to enjoy these masters together for too long. By September, we each had our own teacher, and they would not see each other until February of 2005. I went away with my tail between my legs with my master by my side, but I could not recover, as fast as she did, from the creation of my Limbo, called loneliness. I believed that my loneliness was because I did not have her. Of course now, I know that is not the truth. The reality is that I did not have ME. These would be very tough months, for both the student and the teacher. I was bitter. I was angry. I was hurting. I did not love myself, and I hated everything and everybody.

"Morris" was trying hard to re-enforce "Zorro's" teachings, and some of his own, but I would have none of that. I would take my anger out on my teacher. I would yell at him for no reason. If my Limbo weren't been so thick and murky, I would have noticed that "Morris" would come and comfort me, play, love me and watch me with those big brown eyes that spelled "I love you, no matter what you do or say. I love you for who you are, now love yourself for the same! I am happy being a dog; you be happy you are human, be happy precisely because you are alive. I enjoy everyday, because the now is all that exists for me, and for you, tomorrow may or may not come, just stay here in the now, the two of us."

I now look back and see that it was exactly what he was trying to communicate, but I was not paying attention, because the creations in my head were more "important." I was defeated and totally controlled by my EGO, my Limbo. And to be honest with you, I did not care if it won. All I wanted was her and nothing else mattered, not even me. Once again, I was in my element. I was hurting and suffering, and I was in company of an old "friend"...loneliness.

During most of those months, "Morris" would suffer my swinging moods and anger displays. My teacher kept coming for more love. He was just happy next to my feet, while I cried and drank. Every once in a while he would get up, lick my tears, and go back and lie down. Any possible lesson that I was supposed to learn went right over my head. I was in a cloud, a cloud of dark smoke. By then I had developed kidney disease; my immune system was over-active and decided to attack my kidneys. However, if I really think back about it, the truth of the matter is that my Limbo, my mind, created stress and was probably the main cause. My mind was a match to the energy of the nephritis. I don't know that for sure. But if you agree that the universe is made of vibrating beings and we are all energy, then you would have to agree with me. Assuming it was not my mind that caused it, then for sure I can tell you that there was a very good reason to just enjoy every day, to wake up and smell the roses, to be grateful for the challenges sent, and to move ahead and start learning from your master. But no, I cursed life. I cursed the Creator. I cursed everyone. Why me? No! What did I do to you, God? I was depressed and in a hole. My energy was very low and negative. I matched my energy with illness, so I got sick. I was not doing my best. I was in total darkness. The message from Morris was totally lost. I was not even angry; it was worse. I was getting what I deserved, because the Universe was matching with my Limbo and basically said, "You want darkness, by all means it is done." I was beating on myself. "Morris'" message was to stop thinking so much, appreciate life, and to feel better. Eventually, I did, and so can you, but for now, "Morris" was just a dog and not a teacher. All because the student was not ready yet. Karma had me in its hands.

Just before I got sick, I was a Detective, with long hours, lack of sleep and high adrenaline; which could have been a factor in my illness too. When I discovered my illness, I requested to go back to Patrol division at the Airport Section. I had to go through some sort of chemotherapy pills, and steroids. I was alone. I was depressed. I was ill, also, the medication made me swell up; I think they call it "moon face." My knees swelled, I had constant cramping. I retained water. And again...I was alone. I did not feel attractive, not that I cared, but I was totally regressing. I walked looking down. I was ashamed of my looks, and I was in total Limbo. This was probably the lowest I have been. Later, I would understand that before the door of spiritual awakening opens, a big fall may precede it. And for sure it happened to me.

When Olivia heard about my illness, we decided to give it another try. I hope it wasn't out of feeling sorry for me, but who knows? As we were trying to give it a shot again, I had decided that Morris needed company, you see, I did not see them as teachers or masters yet. I just thought that "Morris" needed a little friend. So I got "Chubaka", a one-pound furry Yorkie mix. So we now had three masters, but we were not paying attention to the lessons. In reality we were three dogs, and a couple.

My Limbo was worse than ever, and the relationship did not last but three weeks, three weeks, people! I blamed her for everything possible. We fought about things that happened in the past, some of it in the very distant past. We said we forgave each other, but I did not mean it. I did not feel what I feel now when I say I forgive someone. Rancor was a very dominant feeling in my soul.

Looking back, all I really needed was to listen to "Morris", but I was just a dog owner, and he was a lonely dog. A long time would have to pass before I would become a student. But at that time, I was down up to my throat in my Limbo, while "Morris" was enjoying the present moment and not showing any signs of loneliness, because it was me that applied such a title to him. He was enjoying his present moment just by touching everybody's life. He had self-love and plenty of love for others. He was a stepparent to "Chubis", took care of him and loved him from the moment he came. No jealousy, no anger he was all he could be, and full of true happiness and passion. He didn't need company. I needed it. He was, at all moments trying to tell me to be a beautiful soul, enjoy life, enjoy this moment, don't think about your problems or the past. Let go of your "sad" story and just BE. No, I did not listen. Hard headed, I guess.

One lesson that I did learn from him, early on, was the concept of energy, it was so obvious and even in my thick Limbo, and it was impossible not to notice. "Morris" is an expert at smelling and an expert at energy sensing. A total master. He can sense moods and auras, or frequencies very easily. If you have two or more pets, you know what I mean. One is clueless, while the other knows and senses high and low energies. Well, "Morris" is one of those.

I could be coming home, and before I even opened the door, he could, and can, sense my frequency. If my mood was happy, sad or angry, he would react accordingly, either by welcoming me by the door and ready to lick my face and fill me with love, or by hiding in the deepest part of his cage, because my energy was very dense. He knows that so clearly, it' uncanny. That was my first lesson, he was trying to show me the door into vibration reading, but my Ego was telling me to push OUT, open the door outwards onto the world, for learning, but geez!! So stupid!! The door out of your mind and into energy.... opens INWARDS! If you want to know yourself, you have to visit your own house.

So obviously I was yet to find the message "I have to go inside of me to find all the love and happiness we all need." My Limbo was fighting. It had me under its grasp, and it wasn't going to let me go easy. Why? Because the first step into waking up is awareness. Awareness of your downfalls, addictions, unhappiness, stresses, or self-rejections. Nevertheless, even after I noticed "Morris' "capacity to read energies, his capacity to read my moods and how his reactions directly correlated to my frequency, my Limbo would take over and put into my mind, all the garbage I had been living with. "Morris" was telling me, "See your Limbo, become aware, see your emotions, and notice how your energy affects me, so obviously it affects all others. Change your energy and you will attract like energy. If you really can train yourself to focus your energy into what you want and not what you don't want, your world would flip. You want to suffer? Suffering shall come. You want love? Then feel love inside you, give love to all, express love, act with love, and love will come to you. Just simply change your frequency, and LET YOUR DOG OUT! If you could only learn that."

Later on, I would get his message, but for now my Limbo was way ahead and was winning.... but just for now.

"Morris" is an old soul. He is unfailingly in balance and constantly centered. He has shown me the beauty of self-acceptance. He accepts himself completely, whether it is about his looks, his weight, his situation at the moment, his pack, his food, everything. He does not show any particular preference. He goes with the flow. It seems that 'it is what it is' goes very well with him, as it should for the rest of us. He is joyous yet he does not go searching for it; rather he finds it in the present-day moment. Every present-day moment is a cause for celebration, since it is the only moment that really exists, as is how we all should live. It is as if he wakes up already deciding that this is the best day ever, but so it will be tomorrow. Give him a little treat, and he shows the utmost gratitude, as does a short walk or a rub on his belly. He enjoys the little things, and so should we. He is always truly "present," and what I mean by truly is that he is "here," he is in the "now" and all of it is a "gift"; which, by the way, in the English language means "present" and so we should be. By the way in Spanish is also the same; "presente" means, both, "gift" and "now".

"Morris" gives me unconditional love, with open heart, and no desire to change me, or others. He is content with who he is, with life as it comes and always coming from love; just as we all should be. He, even at 11 years old, approaches life with enthusiasm. I can't help it to be magnetized by his demeanor. In other words, he is always balanced and harmonized. He is always "OUT," just as you should be.... allow your dog out.

# CHAPTER 4

# Master Chubaka

"Chubis", as we like to call him as a term on endearment, was born sometime in January. The veterinarian decided that January 3rd was good enough. I suspect that he was younger, give or take a week or two. I found him by doing a lot of searching on the Internet, and eventually stumbled on an adoption web site. I found that he was the single survivor of a litter, in which the owner had hung the parents and the rest of the litter, including "Chubis". When he was rescued, he was the sole survivor, barely. The act of that person was beyond forgiveness, at least for my Limbo at the time of his adoption.

Today I know that like attracts like, I might never know how the Universe takes care of the cruelty he imposed against him, but today I forgive him in my heart and in my soul. Someday the laws of the Universe or the human laws will make sure all of Karma descends on him. And you know? Maybe it has already happened, I just don't know or care to know.

When I got Master "Chubis" from the airport in Southern Nevada where he was flown in from Illinois, or was it Michigan? oh well... he was less than one pound, and he could fit in the palm of my hand. His hairy, flat face made it easy to choose his name. However, as time would go on, his name would fit even more, for he was a "dog-human".

When he arrived, he was all playful and energetic. Even so, it was obvious that he had been abused. He was full of fleas. You could feel skin and bones under the fur, and had a big reddish mark around his neck that reminded me of his abuse. No more than two hours later he started to stumble, he appeared to be drugged or really drunk. He was unsteady on his feet, and would fall on his side every time I tried to pick him up. As you can imagine, I freaked out! It was past midnight and only emergency animal hospitals were open. Now I know that his blood sugar was so low that he was about to die. I rushed him to the pet emergency hospital. They told me that there was very little chance that he would survive, but in order to give him his best chance, it would cost over one thousand dollars for the night, and plug him into an IV.

At that time, I was operating without Limbo, so obviously I said, "Do what you can, money is not a problem." Was it a problem? Looking at my checking account ...probably. However, the Universe gave me the answer, and I trusted the response. Here was this little thing depending on my decision, to survive. He had cost me less than 200 dollars to fly him to me, but there was no hesitation on my decision. It was not about the money. It was about love, love for all God's creation. The next morning I took him to "Morris'" and "Zorro's" veterinarian. He had survived the night, but was very, very weak, and needed further care from another doctor.

The vet told me that he had to keep him for a couple of days, and it would be another 700 dollars; I mention this to you, not because I gave a hoot about the money, because I didn't. But because the Universe provides in the time of need, as long as you operate outside the Limbo. Nevertheless, because I was in fact operating totally outside Limbo, and there was no question what my answer was. Of course! The Universe provided!. Somehow the balance in my account was a little higher than it was suppose to be, I got a refund for an overpaid bill, and I tightened my belt for a few weeks.

GEEEEEZ!!! I got a huge lesson right there, and then went back to my old self. But you see, we all get messages here and there. The Universe, God, or whatever you want to call it, is always sending signals of goodness, because goodness is all there is, but we miss them. We are so deep in the voice in the head; in the Limbo creating assumptions, and stories about our life and everybody's life, that we just don't care that life is trying to be a friend to us.

"Chubis" recovered, and I could bring him home. He had zero social skills with either humans or other dogs...so HE made a choice and decided to be more human than a dog. Playing with master "Morris" and/or "Zorro" was a very rare and fantastic sight, but it would only last for a minute. In general, he would ignore them to be with any human, but I became his favorite, and later Olivia, who would wrap him inside her t-shirt while she would vacum the house, it was so funny.

Another lesson was there in front of us. His message said "I was abused. I was almost killed. I was unloved. I suffered. I was in pain. My family was taken. I am anti-social, so what? I am here now. I live in the now, and now is beautiful. I love everyone, for my past is my past and there is where it will stay, is over and is done. The present moment is what counts and just the fact that I am alive is enough to be happy. I give love without conditions or regrets. I give love because I feel like giving it. I am blessed, and I am perfect."

Well, I totally agree now that I sit here writing, but I didn't get it then. Can you imagine a human having gone through all that pain and suffering? That would have been one messed up human. It reminded me of the few stories that I knew about my dad. He probably had all of "Chubis'" issues and believe me, "Chubis" was balanced. While my father was a soul totally lost in his Limbo, because he carried his past as luggage. Luggage with a chain attached to his mind, body and soul. And I wasn't that far behind.

You see,we tend to punish ourselves mentally, all the time. We go through the same story over and over and over again. Then our "loved" ones, remind us of it over and over and over again. We pay for our past not once, but many, many, many times over. If I see my masters, I don't ever recall seeing any of them bite one another today, for the toy they didn't get yesterday. They pay once, then they move on. Let go of the past, the past is just the tail that you drag, but if you see a dog without a tail, it is still a dog. Your past never, ever dictates your present. You are perfect. You were born perfect. You are God, and heaven is a choice. You don't have anything to prove to anyone. The people are living in their own hell, and all it is, is a bunch of lies that your Limbo or ego is throwing your way to keep you under control.

"Chubis" never pretended to let go of his past and put a mask for us to see, he truly let go, and that is the key...Don't pretend your past is gone, to pretend is to wear a mask over the pain you feel; just t don't try to understand what happened to you and why, don't study it or go to a doctor to get a happy-pill.... no! Go beyond, adopt your past, but only the happy memories, believe that you are what you make of yourself now, own your mistakes but don't punish yourself for them, or it will not work. The flaw of looking back is that it drags you into painful memories, those trigger bad emotions, and those emanate bad energy. Why would you want to go there? "Chubis" didn't. His world is in the present moment not where he was.

You might wonder how to do it... I did too, but it wasn't until I had total blind faith that we are God, we are always perfect. We were born perfect, look at any child under 3, look at your pets, "Morris", "Chubis", "Zorro". They sleep if they want to, they play if they want to play, they let themselves just BE. They are authentic, and living in the now. The key is to be aware of the voice in your brain, the voice of the Limbo. Once you are aware of the Limbo, it has very little power. Be aware of the thoughts you have and watch them, see how ridiculous your thoughts are; they are assuming, causing conflict, criticizing, judging, abusing. Limbo cannot survive in the present, or in silence. Look at the masters, and LET YOUR DOG OUT!

Another lesson that "Chubis" was to teach me came one day that I was heading out for a run in the desert. My intention was to run with "Morris" and to carry "Chubis" as we went. He was still barely 3 pounds, and the run was through very rough terrain, full of dunes, thorns, bushes. This was "Morris'" and I, usual run, and I was not expecting this little thing to participate, nor had I wanted him to do so. Paternal love I guess. "Chubis" had a very different idea though. As soon as we got to the desert, I released "Morris", he took off like a rocket, and I followed at my own pace. "Morris" would stop every so often to make sure that I was coming. The terrain was very rough. My pace was slow because my ankles were twisting on the rocks after every few paces. As I ran, with "Chubis" in my arms, he started to bark. He had this particular bark, different from others, is a demanding bark, is a bark that says, "Pay attention to me and understand what I am trying to say, and I want you to do it now!" Well, he was also twisting in my arms. Not hard to figure it out, he wanted down. He was not going to be prevented from joining in the fun, so...I let him down. My Limbo was already putting limitations for him, in my head. No, he can't make it; no, he is too little; no, he is too young; no, he is fragile. Well let me tell you my friends, that day in the desert I cried. That day in the desert I was humbled, and I was in awe. This little piece of fur was running as hard as his little legs would let him... he was so small that his tummy almost touched the ground. Every so often, I would stop to take off the thorns and twigs from his legs and tummy. He would look at me as if saying, "Are you finished because I want to keep running?" "Chubis" would take off after "Morris" again.

"Chubis" never saw himself as too small, or too stupid or too weak. Those words do not exist in the dog's mind. It was me placing these limitations. If "Chubis" was human, he would have believed me, and I would have limited his life, just because of my Limbo beliefs. And that is exactly what a lot of parents do to their children. They place limitations upon them with the excuse that is out of love. In the meantime, you have a child who grows with low self-esteem, and all kinds of messed up excuses to live life. A human "Chubis" would have tried maybe one time, if at all, and then say, "Please Daddy carry me." But not "Chubis", not him. He went on and on. He never stopped trying, even though we ran several miles. He never did less than his best. He never gave up, and he never quit.

When we stopped running I could not contain my tears, I was openly crying and laughing at the same time. What a beautiful lesson I learned in the dessert, that day. I was totally outside my Limbo, egoless, in Heaven, in Joy, in Love.

Doing our best is always enough, our real best. Try, and if you fall...get up and try again. Success has been defined as getting up one more time than you have fallen. Never, never give up. Don't make excuses or lies. It is never about who wins or who loses, is about doing your very best. It is about looking into your eyes in the mirror and being honest with yourself and saying, "Yes. I gave all I got and more." We are always a winner when we do our best. Our best living, our best when we depart this physical body, our best in love, our best in our spirit.

"Chubis" did his best, no doubt about it. "Morris" and my run became "Chubis'" lesson. A lesson for life, a lesson for all, a lesson for us. "Chubis" really LET HIS DOG OUT, and allowed me to let mine out also. Never, ever, ever let someone tell you that you cannot do something or chase a dream. Go get it.

As "Chubis" grew up into this incredibly beautiful dog, he had this incredible six tones of brown and blonde, as if he had gone to an expensive salon for highlights; it was impossible not to notice his beauty interior and exterior. He was so full of love and loved to be loved. I will never forget those hypnotizing eyes. An idea came into my head, and I decided that it would be great to have some of "Chubis" babies. So I went looking for his "girlfriend." Besides, if I was getting so much love from two, then three would be even better. As I was still looking for her in different websites, I can tell you that I was in another era of dark Limbo, and Olivia and I had split up for the second time. The story was the same, jealousy, lies, and possessiveness from my part. I have no idea how she put up with me.

During this time, "Chubis" and "Morris" tried to make a big impact as teachers, but you see, it is only when you are ready for help that you notice the help. Teachers are all around us but they only "appear" when we are ready. And I wasn't. Nevertheless, my masters had stirred something inside me. Something was about to happen inside me.

I reached out to the Church, thanks to my friend "Dani", and the Bible. She encouraged me to go with her but never put pressure for me to learn or believe. I received many beautiful messages there, and a tiny light had come in. I had no problem with many of the messages inside the Bible, but I was in complete discord about their interpretation. Something inside was telling me that God was not for a few that decide to follow this or that religion, but God is for all, inside us. My mind was open for information and peace, so I followed along with it for a while since I was in Peace. The Bear was asleep. I would read passages of the Bible and tried to interpret them with an open mind, rather than a religious mind.

Nevertheless, the longer I listened to some of the sermons the more I disagreed. Especially about certain "rules" that you had to follow, or you would not make it into the Rapture, such as no sex before marriage, Catholicism is a sham, etc. My mom, a devoted Catholic, but more importantly a really true great human being, was not being considered into Heaven according to this church's rules. I had learned enough and now I needed to follow my own path. I was thankful for the peace I had inside, but my spiritual journey was just starting. I chose a different route, and the spiritual wheels started to turn. Nevertheless, thank you "Dani" for the lessons, now my spirit was ready for deeper learning.

While going through this changes, I had found "Trece". She was coming!. Today beautiful "Chubis" has passed on from body into energy. He has joined my father and my mother. He died at eight years of age of anemia. Usually, anemia comes from lack of nutrition. He was always a picky eater, so you had to watch him to make sure he ate. He was living with Olivia when he died. I don't know if "Chubaka" found the diabetic diet for "Zorro", unlikable, or what happened. I cried when I received the news from my Adriana. You will be remembered "Chubis". Thank you for the lessons. Thank you for living your life, your way, every single day. You loved life. You loved all people even if you did not know them. Namaste

# CHAPTER 5

## SHE-Master Trece (13 in Spanish)

"Trece", born December of 2006. I found her on a puppy-website photographed next to a soda can. She was smaller than the can! She was on sale with a big discount, and it looked like nobody wanted her. Maybe because she looked really skinny, and her lower teeth were so prominent. She is a mix of Yorkie and a Pekinese. She has big brown eyes and a funny flat face. I had to have her. This little thing came to me weighing 1 1/2 pounds. She was playful and very well socialized with humans and other dogs, but "Chubis" wanted nothing to do with her. It was not human, so "Chubis" did not see her as part of "his" kind. "Chubis" was there for humans and daddy "Morris", and she was none of them. Did "Trece" mind? Of course she did not.

There was another lesson coming. You see, we as humans tend to take everything very personal. "I am ignored. My ego is hurt, so now I don't like you back." What a lie, we all have what we need right here inside us, in our heart, in our spirit. If "Trece" were human, she would have ignored "Chubis" back, judge him, criticize him, take it personal and maybe even attack him. However, she is not, so no ego came into the equation. By having no ego, she did not take anything personal. She was not affected by "Chubis'" attitude; her demeanor was the same towards him. She would play with me, "Morris" or even "Chubis" with the same enthusiasm. She showed me how, when you don't take anything personal, our lives flow. There is no heavy burden trying to impress, or be liked, or be accepted. She is who she is and that is enough for her. She gave love regardless of how much she got back. She could feel that through her love, she would get it back, but if it didn't, it was still all well in her world. She has no Limbo so is not contaminated with a false story or a sad story. She is who she is. No role to play at all.

I continued to watch their behavior towards each other or me. It was an example of a peaceful and easy life. It is as if she was trying to say that only through love, you will get it back. And even if you don't get it from "them", there is plenty within. Perhaps you will not be a hundred percent successful with all others but through the vehicleof hate the success rate would probably drop to zero. At the same time, she respected the other dog's space, therefore asking for the same in return. Until "Chubis" warmed up to her, she was friendly from a distance, and up close and personal with the rest of us. Of course the character of my dogs, it is "my" version of what they are. I created "their" life according to my filters, but in reality, they are who they are, and I am who I am, period. I realized that I don't really know who I am or who anybody else is. I have a version of the people in my life, and they have a version of who I am, but both are lies, created completely by our limbos. First of all, because I really don't know anybody and second, because we consistently find ourselves playing roles. The role of the pet owner, the cop, the boyfriend, the parent, the client, the boss, the victim, etc. We are unfailingly trying to fit in, impress, be accepted, so we lose who we truly are and play fake roles. My Masters love me, and each other, for whom we are. They walk proudly as dogs, and they don't suffer from an identity crisis. They respect me as well as each other. They don't have to ask permission to eat or sleep. They do it when they feel like it. There are no rules about it, and even when they get upset at each other, their reaction is immediate, fast and there are no resentments.

Humans, depending on who they are, jump immediately on one another and most often over react, and then they judge you and hold grudges, sometimes for the rest of their lives. Others, are afraid to react but there is anger bottled up inside, for a long, long time. They curse you in their mind and even get sick from holding onto this hate towards another fellow human. And worst of all, humans hold the biggest grudges against those closest to them, as if they are owed something.

When "Trece" was about eight months old, she came into "heat." She was ready (physically) to have babies, but probably it was not the best time to get pregnant according to books, because she was too young and all her instincts were not fully developed, but I did not know that. And since I saw "Chubis" pay zero interest in being a friend to "Trece", my Limbo turned its back to Nature. I assumed (wrongly) that nothing would happen.

So sex happened. A double-edged word. Why? Because depending on who is reading it, the word itself will bring different reactions into the mind of the reader. Some people would rather avoid the subject because they were taught that sex is wrong, or dirty, or only made for married people, etc. Others would love to hear about it hopefully because they know is natural, beautiful and fun. Others will want to hear about it because it's a taboo, but a dirty secret that they want to hear with morbid ears. All depends on your perception to these three letters. However, you see, your version of sex is just an image based on your past experiences with it. All of it is a lie. Not a lie that you had a particular good or bad experience, but such experiences should stay there, in the past. The fresh experience is that, just a brand new experience of the now. But humans develop mental problems and ideas, as well as burdens and worries created by your mind to which many, or most, are not true. Most of these ideas are created from a past that never occurred, or if it occurred was not quite as devastating as we remember them. Conversely, they are worried about a future that is not here, nor we know if it will ever occur as we think about it. Sex is just a vehicle to express love, but we were programmed by our Limbo families and friends to think of it as taboo, as a weapon, as a toy, as a past time, as filth, as unspeakable. All are lies of course, but we believe them and we applied them to what we call our morals, and we use the word sex as a scapegoat of some of our suffering.

Some people use sex as a replacement of love, or as a unique sign of love. Some others use it for attention, some because they were victims, some because they are abusers, some as a weapon of superiority and some others to fill their insecurities or loneliness. In other words, some people have sexual encounters when they are not in alignment, while "Chubis" and "Trece" were in complete alignment, and it was natural and beautiful.

I am not here to say that you should go out there and have sex whenever or for whatever reason, quite the contrary, what I am saying is that anytime you are in alignment with your spirit, the sex will be more enjoyable. Having sex without an agenda or without taboos is much more enjoyable than when you have a voice in your head telling you why or what the conditions of why or why not, you should have sex. In other words, do it out of respect to yourself without an underline motive. Take your ego out of the act, or any action. Do not allow your Limbo to control you, if you are successful, the joy automatically will be there, especially if your partner is coming into the act, with the same pure mind. "Chubis" and "Trece" for sure Let Their Dog Out, and puppies were on their way.

By the time "Trece" got pregnant, Olivia and I were back together one more time. It was like we could not stay away from each other. The laws of energy and vibration were clearly showing us that we had the same dense energy attracting each other. But there was something that she did not count on, my Limbo; my darkness was less thick, less murky. I had been alone for nearly one year, and I had used it to study not only my Masters, but also whom I call my Super-Masters, in the likes of Eckhart Tolle, Abraham Hicks, Dr. Wayne Dyer, and Don Miguel Ruiz. I also read passages of the Bible with Dani, The Tao and several Buddhist teachings. I was by no means awakened or enlightened, but there was a shift occurring in my spirit.

One of the things that I had not been able to change was the belief that she was a necessity in my life; that we were made for each other, that my complete happiness was dependent on our relationship. So for a while our comeback seemed like the perfect and logical result. My Limbo was not controlling me as much as before, so we had many moments of fun and laughter. I trusted myself, and my confidence was up again. What I did not know is that my Limbo appeared to have grown thicker and darker in different areas, or at least, that's how it felt compared to before.

Time went by and I found myself in my Limbo riding Heaven, not real Heaven, but I felt totally alive. Trece's pregnancy brought a lot of lessons. One of them was in how to be a parent. I gave her the freedom to be herself while at the same time I took care of her, bathed her, and gave her vitamins. I studied puppies' birth and prepared myself for the upcoming babies.

I have a son; his name is "Man". I tried to be more of a friend to him, since I could only see him every two weeks, when he was young. I was not a real parent because I was angry and depressed while going through parenting. I did not want to be a dad. My freedom was gone. I was not tolerant of any tantrum, which was logical given the situation of the divorce between his mom and I. I now know that I had to mind my own business and allow him to flourish on his own. I would have been a better parent if I had tended to my own Limbo, instead of interrupting his growth, especially coming from my darkness. But that is another story all on its own.

On October 17th, three babies came in this world. It happened to be Olivia's birthday also, so I was so ecstatic, it was a sign! I had three babies on her birthday! "Trece" announced the pup's birth by nesting in the whelping pen I had built next to my bed. When she went into labor, I was totally in the zone, no ego, fully into the present moment. I was so full of love and peace at the same time. Being in the zone is how all should be most of the time. Totally immersed in the now. The difference between what we call an awakened person and the rest of us is not something extraordinarily complicated or time consuming. It is rather, the ability to remain in the Now.

Make peace with where you are, who you are with, what you are doing, and pay your complete attention to it. By making peace with the present moment and being 100 % into it, gives zero chance to the voices in the head to give way to past or future, real or imagined, situations. The voices have to be quiet, and by being quiet you are acting under the direction of your heart and not the ego. You are awakened. You are enlightened. What does that mean to us? It means that at one point or another, all of us have experienced moments of enlightenment. All we have to do is be aware of how we did it. And go back there whenever we want.

I can promise you that, even though I don't know you, probably you were in an awaken status while creating art, during a dangerous situation, observing beauty, exercising, playing music, dancing etc. Maybe you don't know that you were awakened, but you were. Your mind was quiet, and you were acting by instinct or following your imagination and heart. Just like our dogs would do. We all have the tools to be awakened already, all we have to do is go into our toolbox and use them, and then get ready to Let Your Dog Out.

"Trece" was so young when she was giving birth, that she had very little notion on what to do. Her instinct told her to nest, to regulate her breathing, to push with the contractions. Yet, she was so little that she looked scared and tired. The first puppy to be born was "Peanut," a name given to her by their eventual new owner. "Trece" knew by instinct that she was supposed to eat the placenta, so she did so. But she did not know that she was supposed to clean the puppy and chew on the umbilical cord, so I cut it for her. I rubbed the puppy, extracted any mucus from its throat and cut the cord. I was not certain how many puppies were inside her, and I was not confident how much time would go in between births, so we waited patiently. About 2 minutes later, "Trece: was ready to deliver number two. The second puppy to come and also the biggest of the three was "Lobo". She was obviously having trouble giving birth, maybe because he was bigger than the first one. Olivia, who was present during this process, suggested to help her by pressing against her stomach. So while she pushed, I pulled on the puppy. It was slippery and "Lobo" was refusing to come out. After a while, I could get a hold of "Lobo" and pull him out. Unlike "Peanut" who was wrapped in the normal one birth sack, "Lobo" was wrapped in two. I placed "Lobo" next to "Trece" to see if she would do her job on her own, but again she was only interested in eating the second placenta. I then ripped the first sack, ripped the second sack, and started rubbing "Lobo's" body. He was limp and lifeless. I sucked the mucus from his throat and continued rubbing his body for what seemed an eternity. Finally, "Lobo" came to life, and started crying and moving around.

Let me tell you I have no training in how to do what I did. I was just totally in the Zone. I let my actions be dictated by heart and instinct. I was crying by the beauty of the birth process, by the fact that "Lobo" was alive and by the energy of love coming from these moments. It appeared that "Trece" was done giving birth. I felt her tummy and she felt empty, in addition to the fact that she was worn out and was falling asleep. Olivia felt "Trece's" stomach, and her motherly instincts were telling her that another pup was still inside. This time Oli and I had to give birth for "Trece". She was worn out and was not helping at all. Oli pushed on "Trece"'s stomach in a downward motion, and as soon as I saw the pup's head coming out, I started to pull. Baby number 3 was born. "Botitas" was born!!! He was black with white socks. Wow! What an amazing experience that was. The miracle of life right before our eyes.

"Trece" was not very helpful giving birth but being a mother came easy and immediately. She assumed her role right away. After she had rested, she started cleaning the pups by licking them. She encouraged their vowel movements and only left her pen when she had to go potty. She loved her puppies all the same, right away. She looked at them and seem to count them up every time she had to come back to them, it was total and complete love, no judgments, no limitations, and an awesome mother.

However, instead of learning the lesson of love inside of all of us, we always say that it is a mother's love. As if a mother's love was special or unique, or different. I know I run a big risk by saying this, but feeling special for being a mother is a creation of your ego. It feels special because it is similar to a puppy love. Pure and authentic. The only reason that a mother's love looks special and unique is because it comes from a pure place. This love is totally in alignment with the Universe. This love is pure; it is clean energy. We tend to look at it as special because we believe that we cannot love the same, unless you are a mother. That is NOT true. We all can love one another in the same way by having clean vibration. By lining up with the present, by being compatible energetically to your spirit. By acting without Limbo. By Letting Your Dog Out. But the only way to get there is to have a "mother's Love" for us first, and for the world next.

As the weeks went by, I noticed how the babies developed their own personalities. "Peanut" was the smallest of all of them and also the first one to go to a new owner. He was about eight weeks old. I now had two puppies left, "Lobo" and "Botas". I wanted to keep "Botas" because he was black and white, and "Lobo" was golden and that was the only color of the dogs we had. I knew I could not keep them both, so I had to decide. My love for both was the same so I decided by color.

Nevertheless, the new owner refused to take "Lobo" because he wanted the short-legged "Botas". At the same time, Olivia was not in agreement that I wanted to keep another dog. I tried to explain that for the first time we were going to have a homegrown pup, who also happened to be born on her birthday. Since I wanted to keep "Botas" and sell "Lobo", I finally tried to compromise with her by giving her the choice on which one she preferred. She said "Lobo" because, as she put it, he was similar to her. Feisty, independent, and always getting into trouble. She loved that about him. So the decision was made. "Botas" left, and "Lobo" stayed.

Soon after "Lobo" was born, I moved to Olivia's house, with my tiny pack of masters. I helped her brother erect a front yard fence, so they would have the small back porch, plus access to the front lawn without escaping. At this time, it seemed like my world was coming together nicely. My Limbo was asleep, like a bear in hibernation but sometimes very awake. It was a roller coaster. One cold January morning, our lives collided and a war of two worlds had erupted. It would not be the last time, but it seemed very much like a final episode. What happened?

As my Limbo laid asleep but not dead, she told me that she believed I was having an affair, after checking my phone for signs of unfaithfulness. What she found was a text from a friend and only a friend, who happened to use the word 'sweetheart' as part of her everyday lingo. That was enough for the break-up. We argued and my Limbo woke up. I reacted by getting into her face; yelling, screaming that she was wrong, and that she could call my friend and ask her. She told me her feelings and, once she was finished saying her peace, she went into the bedroom and locked it. I needed to say my peace and defend myself, so I went after her. When I noticed that the door was locked, I kicked it many times until I made a hole enough to slide my arm through and open it. I was angry, but all I wanted was to talk. As I entered the room, I noticed that she was on the phone with 911, telling the dispatcher that I had hit her, that I had a gun and that I was a policeman. I knew there was no way that I could talk to her now. I put my shoes on, and left in my car.

That night or early morning (it was about 2 am), I realized that I had no real friends. I texted a few of the numbers I had on my phone to see if I could stay in their couch, but nobody responded. I went and parked at the parking lot of a nearby establishment. After a few minutes, a Police Sergeant left me a message on my phone to attempt to convince me to come back to the house and tell him my side of the story. I went back.

You should have seen the scene outside her home. There were over seven police cars, including a Lieutenant, a Sergeant, five patrol officers, and a few minutes later three cars with plain clothes detectives. It looked like a homicide scene or some major crime had occurred. As I went inside I was asked to sit in the front leaving room while they spoke with her and her daughter. They took my gun for safe keeping, photographed the damage to the door, took a report with taped statements from both women, and then finally they were ready to speak to me.

I went with a detective to his car, and once inside he read me my rights and asked several questions, including whether I had touched her in anyway. Of course that was a big no, so I told the truth. After a few minutes the detectives told me that I was not being arrested for lack of evidence (no injuries to her face), and it was nice of Olivia and her daughter to tell the truth after the situation was calmed, so I was free to leave but the police had a strong recommendation (almost an order) that I had to stay somewhere else for the night. I agreed, so I left without knowing where to go.

I drove with no sense of direction for what seemed hours, but I am not sure. Later that morning I came back to the house, parked outside and tried to sleep in my car. I guess I dozed off, because when I open my eyes it was morning. I went into her house, and she was already awake, or who knows what kind of night she had. She looked at me and said "You have two days to move out or I will put a restraining order on you, and you will have to move anyway." All I said was "OK."

I went to the store to get as many boxes as I could, to pack my belongings. I rented a storage room, and slowly, without any help, I moved what I could into it. There was a lot of furniture that I decided to leave behind, since I could not carry it but mostly because I did not want her to have nothing left. Two days later, I moved. During the move, I texted every single person I knew to attempt to rent floor space from them. Everyone I tried did not answer or said no, except an old friend, whom I had not kept in touch with, but when she saw my text immediately said yes. Thank you "Tash", I will never forget what you did. Of course, I had to leave my masters behind.

Olivia was kind enough not to blame my dogs for what she was blaming me for, and said that she would take care of them as long as necessary. Looking back at the incident that precipitated my move, I now know that my reaction was wrong. I tried to fight fire with fire. I felt accused unjustly for something I did not do and my ego got hurt. When my ego felt attacked, I unleashed my Limbo against hers, and the results were not surprising. I should have responded with understanding for her hurt, with compassion for her wild Limbo and with Love at all times. But of course at that time it was easier said than done. I was completely under the spell of my monster, and it would not let me go. I left her home, not knowing what the future would bring but with the firm realization that I had to change. I had to conquer my Limbo, or I was going to go down hill. I had to Let My Dog Out, without my dogs. One more time, all those lessons of love and patience from "Trece", had gone over my head.

Now a days "Trece" has an awesome approach to life, she is slow and deliberate in all her action. She truly has mastered the walking-meditation. She goes at it very slow, and stopping often to explore her surroundings. She is also very independent and prefers to stay in her little house than in anyone's company. She is not lonely, but prefers to be alone and comfortable in her paws. She is a very wise master.

LET YOUR DOG OUT

PARIS - LAS VEGAS

# CHAPTER 6

## Letting My Dog Out

As I start this chapter, you might be asking why I decided to skip the chapter about my other master, "Lobo". I skipped his story because most of his lessons came after "I Let My Dog Out," but I will let you know about his lessons soon. Let me back up a bit. I went to "Tash's" home with a couple of bags of clothes and whatever I needed to be active in this world. It's funny how we are pack rats collecting things for life, then something happens in your life, and you find that surviving in this world with the very minimum of things its not so bad and you don't really need all that extra stuff.

I will forever be grateful to "Tash" for opening her home to me. People that were much closer to me during this time completely turned their back to me. However, the Universe never leaves you to die out there, especially when you are trying and asking to manifest help. At the time that I was going through my challenges, without having any knowledge about the Law of Attraction, I recall so clearly that I was asking to "God" for help and to create a savior. And I was asking from a place of peace and aliveness, while the desired outcome was already a feeling throughout my body. Somehow I knew deep inside that the Universe would provide. I was at peace and my friend opened her home to me. It was a short stay at her house. First because I knew that I needed a place where I could have my masters back and second because I needed time for myself and not in someone else home.

Nevertheless, I made the best out of it. Besides the time that I had to use for going to work, I dedicated myself to reading and exercising. I did not go out too much. I did have fun going out, but I was at a place in life where my thinking had improved, was clearer, I was no longer playing a role. I was being me. Me the spiritual being and not identifying myself with the role of this or that. One night that I decided to go out, I got a text from a friend who invited me to meet him at a restaurant. During this night, I met one of the greatest human beings out there. "Tina".

I remember being seated at the bar and all of a sudden the energy in the room changed for the better. "Tina" had walked in. I immediately recalled how "Morris" reads my energy. I was doing the same. I was reading the energy that surrounded her. Even though we did not speak too much, I could sense her energy of happiness, friendliness and good vibe. It was as if I could see an aura surrounding her. Her laugh is also very contagious and honest, and it is good that she laughs often and freely. Before she left she handed me her card and told me to call her sometime. I did call and "Tina" and I became instant friends.

Most of our conversations were very deep, interesting and spiritual. We spoke about relationships, life and how we all humans have learned patterns, and we assigned those thoughts as who we are. I was awakening, and life was getting very exciting. I had realized that the Universe had placed her in my path, so the lessons from my Masters could have a voice. My dogs had tried to teach me so many lessons, the same way they pass them to one another, but I could not get it, so the Universe said, "Here is" Tina "...now listen! And Let Your Dog Out."

The voice of my angel was here. Just at the precise moment that I needed it. She showed me movies such as "The Celestine Prophecy," "Radio," "Conversations with God," and "Facing the Giants." She allowed me to listen to Tony Robbins tapes and showed me a couple of books that would help me, especially Louise Hay. While on my own, I was following Dr. Dyer and trying to understand Eckhart Tolle. I was getting messages from all directions and in every form. I was getting messages even from songs and poems. I had lost my relationship, but I was finding myself. I was staying in the present moment at most times, and I was beginning to understand that I was not the voice in the head and that awareness of the voice would help me quiet the mind or at least not to follow the string of thoughts forever with no end. I felt gratitude, and I felt very rich. I was aligned during most of the time. I accepted my situation and life.

I guess you could say that a "little puppy" wanted to come out. The first time I let my first dog out is when I found myself knowing that I had forgiven me and my relationship, my dad, and any of those characters that had made my life difficult in my eyes. But then again, what I had realized was that nobody had made my life hell...I had made my life hell through my mind, my thoughts, my memories and my resentments. I finally understood that the reason why my Dogs always forgave me was because they had "paid no mind" to it. They have no reason to remember wrong doings by others. They don't think; they don't hold grudges because it is your memory of events and the re-living of past events it's what fuels our anger towards someone. It was so amazing to feel with no resentment or hate for no one. I surrendered to my inner peace, to the quiet and blissful silent in my head.

Nevertheless, my Limbo was not going to go quietly, and it would try and try again to get me to fall back into and ego dominated life. All this time I found myself battling the voice in the head. The battle between staying in the Now or being dominated by the thoughts in my head, which usually are about the past or a future event, that may or may not happen. Yes, my shift was coming along but the steps were "baby steps." Why? Because I was not getting the full message, not from my Dogs, not from the books. I was not ready. I was still trying to open the door to awakening towards the outside. I was pushing and pushing, and it would not open. If I had only tried to pull the door inwards maybe I would have found ME a lot sooner, but I was not doing it, and my learning had to go on for a while longer.

I started to see how my health, good or bad, was related to my state of mind, so I followed the path of positive incantations, telling myself in front of the mirror that I loved myself, that I am perfect and that all is good in my life. It worked a little bit. It worked because my mood was better, and I smiled more often, but it didn't completely work because I did not know the secret, the secret that you have to believe it, feel it and refuse the evidence of reality and stay with your belief.

So all of you out there reading, I ask you please, that if you are going to practice incantations, which I recommend, you should go deep into your heart and really love yourself. Later on, I will explain how I went beyond incantations, but as a first practice it does work. Why? Because even though you can't stay out of your mind, might as well use it to nurture and love yourself.

Dogs love themselves and have confidence in themselves not because they repeat incantations into their head, but then again, they were lucky enough to be born without a mind, so they do it by instinct. But, again, for those of us that are trapped in the head, incantations serve a purpose. And if done well, you can actually perform in the "normal" world in quite a joyful way. It is not enlightenment, but is a very good "feel good" technique. If you combine the incantations with proper body posture, they work even better. What you do is use your body in a dynamic way. You smile. You talk with energy. You walk straight, head up, shoulders back. Yes, it works, trust me, I tried it. It is not enlightenment either, but you do feel better. I tried to feel depressed while walking with energy and my head up...and I couldn't. Look at your Dog. How do they walk? Their tail is up. The swagger is on. They pulled you. They show complete confidence. Yes, I know that comes naturally to them but if enlightenment is just not happening, this practice is very efficient. Try it and you will understand what I mean. Yes, you are still trapped in the head, but at least you are walking on top of the world.

It is so funny to think back right now how I was not ready for some teachers yet. Eckhart Tolle, Buddha, and the Tao, were soooooo boring to me. I would fall asleep reading them. Why? Because I was not ready for them. So, please don' t be hard on yourself, if as you try different techniques, you find them boring or uninteresting. You will see as your process moves forward, that you will come back to them. I guess enlightenment is boring but today my super masters are Eckhart Tolle and the Buddha. Yes, I went back eventually, when I was ready to move from the outside to the inside, but for now I was doing my practice in the world of form, and it was working in a very comfortable way.

By now, "Tina" had unleashed "my inner angel." I was all over the place looking for spiritual help. I found Don Miguel Ruiz and his "four agreements," I found "The Secret." I went into YouTube to watch Tony Robbins and Abraham Hicks; they are incredible teachers in the world of the mind. They take you exactly where your mind and thoughts should go in order to have happiness follow you wherever you go, without making happiness as a goal but enjoying the journey.

You have to make your own decisions on which school you follow. Try, read, watch, and listen. I was ready for it all, but not yet for Tolle or Buddha, Osho or the Tao. I guess I was into the mind control, and I liked talking myself into feeling good. Today I just feel good. I have gone inside to find the real me in the deepest level. I live in the Now and today my teachers have changed, and I cannot tell you which teacher to follow, that is your own path. I guess in a way I was a thinking dog, which is better than a thinking human. And for now I was OK with it. I was just a spiritual seeker.

As I was feeling so "free" and happy and energetic, I started to feel a sense of urgency to share my learning with anyone whom I might encounter. Does the Dog tell another, "Be in the moment!!" "Enjoy this moment!!" No, they are what they are. So another lesson that I needed to learn was the fact that you don't go out there preaching and teaching to those that do not reach out to you. You teach by your behavior, your energy, and your peace; just like my pack of Dogs do. No lesson, just relax and be yourself, your true self.

Of course, some of my lessons came before I was aware that they were lessons. Awareness has to be your first priority, or you will miss all the beautiful message being sent your way by your dogs, your babies, your pets, nature, or spiritual teachers.

How do you attain awareness? Well, the way I did it was by staying in constant vigilance of what was going in my head: my judgments of others, the direction of my thoughts. You have to be careful. You have to become a watchdog of your thoughts, so you know that the voice in the head is not the "real" you, and you remain undisturbed to whatever is going on in the mind. If you can't remain undisturbed, at least you can watch what is going on, and try to remain unattached, even if a little, from the direction your head is trying to take you. Yes, maybe you will still scream, rant and act crazy, but you saw it. Next time you will see it again. And eventually you will have a little control, then more and more and more; until one day you catch it BEFORE you loose it.

Lessons come to each of us in a different order, with distinct intensity and different consequences. Once you start working on the muscle of awareness, you are allowed to go into the past, only and only for one reason: To collect prior lessons that you might have missed while you were trapped by your Limbo. As long as you can remain completely detached from any feelings and emotions and suffering that the memory might bring, you can go there and collect the lesson. Only the lesson. Once you collect the lesson, you go back to the present. It is very important that you understand that everything I explain in this book is only a pointer directing you towards the door of stillness. Once you are in front of the door it is your responsibility to enter whenever you're ready. It is very probable that you are thinking, "I have memories. I cannot forget my memories." Well, I am not telling you to forget your memories. I am telling you stop being a slave of those memories. The memories you have are usually attached to your Limbo, and your Limbo is trying to drag you down into hurt, and pain. In other words, it wants to hunt you down. And it hunts you down by recalling a bad experience and an emotional reaction, or by worrying about the unknown future and painting it very bleak. If you fall for the trick, the Limbo has you where it wants you. At the same time, the voice says, "I just want the best for myself." But who is "myself?" It is the ego.

You are the one witnessing this conversation. And 99 times out of a 100, what the voice says is just for its convenience, which is to have you under its spell. For example, if somebody asked you what kind of toys you played with when you were 10 years old. The normal response is to go into your memory bank and remember them, visualize the toys and then tell me exactly what they were. You would give me these descriptions without attachment, without Limbo, just memory. No attachment whatsoever. But if somebody asks you, what kind of father did you have, regardless of what kind of father he was, you would describe him with emotion, with feeling, with attachment. Especially if he was an abusive parent. Then you would describe him not only with emotion but also with your particular version. You would recall this person with pain or worse, maybe with hate or you would refuse to remember him. What is happening here is that your Limbo enjoys making you feel bad or sad or emotional. The memory is not doing that, the memory is just there but the Limbo is feeding from your pain. In other words, the purpose that you have is to recall any memory without attachment. But how do you do it? You do it by being present and aware of what your Limbo is trying to make you feel. Once you are aware that the voice is not yourself, but the voice from the ego trying to control you, you can then try to stop the voice. If the voice cannot be quieted, then use the voice to speak only positive sentences about yourself and the world. If you want you can even go to the extreme of saying out loud 'stop-no more', or snap your fingers or create a personalized clue that would wake you up whenever you are immersing yourself in the voice in the head.

You have to understand that this voice is full of lies. If you dropped your story, the Limbo would not survive. Letting your dog out is a slow and painful process, especially if you don't have any masters living with you. You have to "Dog-Up" at your mistakes, take responsibility for them, but not feel guilty; otherwise, they will own you forever.

During this time, I was not living with my Masters. I didn't know if I was ever going to see them again. I was going through my pain all by myself. I was searching for the doors of awareness with a blindfold, and I was going out late, and I was avoiding my true self. I was unhappy one minute, euphoric the next. I was numb one minute, then felt everything, the next.

As the weeks went by, something inside of me started to wake up. I forced myself to go to the gym. I started to speak to myself kindly in front of the mirror. I dressed better, took care of my body, and forced myself to smile. It was so hard in the beginning. I had to love myself again. One day, I woke up, and I told myself "Mauricio, I forgive you," and I meant it. Even my acne cured up, my stress was going down.

Slowly, my life was turning around, from dark days to sunshine. Yet the nights were still a challenge.

Since the split with Olivia, there were mostly dark nights. My days were fun or so they seemed. I was living in the moment; I was smiling, and my body felt great but during the night my Limbo would come back. It was very hard to sleep because I could not keep the voice in my head quiet. My Limbo was saying terrible things inside my head; my imagination was running wild. And my memories with complete attachment were sad and depressing.

As the time passed I was able to ask for my condo back from my renters, and they were willing to move out. It felt good to know that I would have my Masters back. During this time, I got a text from Adriana asking to keep "Chubis." for good. I told her that I would consider it, but I needed to see all of them. When Adriana met me at the park, I said hello and good-bye to "Zorro" and loaded the rest of the dogs. I know she was expecting me to allow "Chubis" to go back with her, but I was far from being enlightened, and I told her that "Chubis came with an owner", and "we both go or no one". I guess I was trying to send a message for Olivia to come back to me. I left the park with a slight smile on my face for my non-existent victory. How pathetic I looked. I was so immerse in my thinking still, that I assigned the title of "victory", to my ridiculous and immature actions.

I started to feel better about my life having my home and dogs back, but at the same time I was hiding behind a mask of fake smiles, nightclubs and easy women. In other words, I was living in dark and in light, separated by the actual time during the day, because during daylight, I was quite positive. I was not talking negative about any situation, and I would constantly hear Ms. Louise Hay on CD, as well as Tony Robbins and Don Miguel Ruiz. I can't say who helped me more during that time. Ms. Hay showed me how to Love myself and repeat it again and again, while driving, at home, or anywhere I thought I needed a push. Tony Robbins gave me so much energy from his up beat voice and positive outlooks, and Don Miguel gave me my first basis into spiritualism, by being easy to read and yet so deep, with four simple agreements that could change anybody's life.

At the same time, I used my memory to remember all those messages of love my Masters had given me and made a promise to myself that I would pay more attention. I was now officially a student, and I was totally committed to my well-being and self-love with the mission of Letting My Dog Out once and for all. I have to tell you that the first time I heard that I was not what I thought, I actually said, "bullshit."

I was so identified with this concept that in order to grasp it, I had to attempt being quiet for a few seconds and see what would happen. Of course, I did not disappear, but it was so hard to remain there, in silence. The other side of this concept is that if you quiet your mind, you will not disappear, but also when the mind is talking, whatever it is saying is ego based, therefore, a lie. Slowly and whenever I remembered, I would analyze what was that I just said to myself. I started to see a pattern...most of the time that my mind was talking was to complain, judge, qualify and quantify my actions, and other people's actions.

Once you start trying this simple exercise, you will realize that it is very useless chatter, or worse, damaging chatter towards yourself or others, or towards situations and things. In other words, you are never where you are. Your mind carries you to other places and time. Pause for a second, wait for your mind to start talking, what is it saying? Am I right? You just made yourself into the Observer, the Watcher, or the Witness for the first time. Try it often, this was the best I could do at the beginning of my journey, since the chatter was always there.

Ephesians 4:32 tells you, "Some people see forgiveness as a weakness – a kind of giving up. But what are we giving up on? Holding on to anger and a grudge? Forgiveness is strength – the strength to let go of the hurt and release it to God. Forgive and be free." And that includes you.

At the level that I was at that time, I told myself that I would try to live each day as if it was my last. So all the challenges and misfortunes that I had suffered, had to be buried. Everything was said and done, no need to keep beating my head against the wall because of it. I also had to realize that today I am as young as will ever be, and not wish for my looks of the prior day, month, year or decade. I can't turn back the time on my body. All of that is gone. Burned. Forgotten.

But at the same time it is not all about the past, it is also about tomorrow. Tomorrow should not be of my concern. It will come when it comes, and it will be today. Forget about the "what if's" or the "maybes." I cannot fully operate today if I am thinking about tomorrow. And what is worse tomorrow is all in our imagination, which might never even come true.

I have to follow my Masters and give a thank you for the sun coming up in the morning. I know that many other humans did not get to wake up this morning, so I was granted a special privilege. Why? Perhaps their journey was finished. I don't know, but I am here. So thank you, Universe, thank you God!

I can't even save any of my life- time, in case I need it, once its gone, its gone. I can't have a reserve of hours to use in case of emergency, so I need to use them all wisely. Not even the richest person can go somewhere and buy time so they can live longer; even those with wealth of money are not allowed this honor. Hence, if I am to live as if my last day, I cannot waste my time with people willing to do nothing. Or to hang out with those that judge all others or all situations. This was one particular thing that I seemed to master, for today I have few friends. I stopped mocking others, or judging them or joining them in the drama of the day. Eventually, I was an outcast. Not that it mattered, for I was living my last day in this life.

I was trying as best as possible to let go of dramas, judgments, and negativity. I don't know if I went at it the right way, what I do know is that I do not miss any of those situations or people, especially at work, that brought me a sense of uneasiness. I guess that would be a signal that I did the right thing. Just as Buddha did, I did not accept their drama, abuse, judgments and negativity; so all these judgments still belong to them. Letting my dog out was fun, yet a lot of work, because I refused to let go of my thoughts. I was still hurt by my split up, and it showed. Yet, I also noticed that I loved myself so much more than I had ever done. And it was during this time that this book was born. A birth that would take many years to finalize.

# CHAPTER 7

## Master Lobo

As I said before, I told you I would get back to "Lobito", born in my home, with "Chubis" as his father, and "Trece" as his mother. Since "Trece" had given birth to three puppies, I was able to distinguish very clearly who was the alpha. Guess who? Yes, "Lobo." He had a difficult birth, but from the moment he was born, he would, literally, push his way around, to get the best food from his mom.

Once he got a few weeks old he would try to rule everyone, and I mean all of us, the adult dogs, the two brothers, and even me. This tiny thing would growl and fight for his place at the top. Of course, everything in life has some sort of rules, and before he could become a master, he had to learn his place in the pack.

Now, I was not going to interfere between the dogs. They had to decide who was who in their pecking order, but with humans, it was very important that I could learn from him, but I was the provider, and he needed to show respect. It took a couple of mini-scuffles to decide a winner. I came on top. It would be 2 years of constant challenges from him, before he gave up completely. Nobody got hurt in the process; in fact, it was very funny to see his challenges, which were never aggressive in nature, just bluff. Eventually, he settled quite well with all of us, but at the same time he always remained independent. One of his obvious challenges to authority was his amazing skill at escaping fences, gates and even cages. He was not born to be held and by golly, he was going to do his hardest to get his point across.

At first, it was frustrating to find him roaming the neighborhood, because I did not want him to be stolen or to get hurt. Just prior to his birth, and roughly seven months from my prior break up, I was back with my Olivia, again. I know, I know. I guess my Limbo won, or I don't know why we did it, but here we were again. As I said before, she was present during the puppies' birth. So a lot of our time we spent at her home. I created a fortress around her house to avoid "Lobo's" escapes. A lot of money was spent in an escape proof yard. But of course he always found his way out. If he wanted out, he was out. Period.

In a big way, this was a great lesson. Never Give Up! Persevere, achieve. It was so funny to see this 10-pound dog literally scaling the 5-foot fence, a little at a time. He would jump up and use his shoulders and rear legs to continue to the top, then balance himself at the top and jump over. Sometimes he was gone for hours but would always come back with a big smile. He would then jump on a power box next to the fence and leap into the yard. This was his way of showing me how to live life. Free, free from fears, free from limitations, free from real or imaginary fences. It is as if he would be saying to me, "Nothing is impossible if you want it bad enough."

We so often place our limitations in our minds, even before we try. How often you hear your Limbo talking to you, saying, "It's too hard," "It's too difficult," "It's too tall, too short, too big, too small," or worse we say, "I'm too stupid," "I can't do that," "Maybe tomorrow," 'It's not for me," "I will never learn," "I'm too old, too young, too ugly", "too much this, too much that." Excuses, excuses, excuses. All these imaginary excuses and judgments that we impose on ourselves are complete lies. Maybe you read these lines and say, "but I am in fact, a fat person". So I say to you, accept it, love yourself and from that foundation. Do something about it, or do nothing. Either way you will be operating from acceptance.

"Lobo" had no excuses, he would try this way, that way, this corner, that technique, try another form. He just would never give up. This game he played was exempt from fear or doubts. I can almost imagine him laughing at my "new" anti-escape device. I could almost hear his spirit saying, "Go ahead, keep trying to limit my capacity to go out. I dare you. I have no limits. I can do what I want, when I want, nothing can stop me. I don't know fear, and I love me. You want to put limitations or conditions to Love? Go ahead. However, I have no limits, no conditions to my Love and my desires. I will stop when I want, if I want, that is how you live life."

I was trying to change him to fit me, just as I did in all of my relationships. At some point or another I always fit my personality to somebody else desires or wants, or vice-versa. Here was "Lobito" showing me, though he loved me, he wasn't going to change just because I said so. All beings in the Universe, animals, humans, change because they want to and not because they have to. Even animals or humans that have been abused, conform with the change to avoid punishment, but not as a real change. Given the opportunity, they would go to be their own self. It is not until the energy they read tells them that a certain change its in their benefit, that they will adhere to it. The change can be sudden and fast, or slower and over time. All depends on what their instinct tells them. Once they read the instinct, they follow it without stopping to analyze it, as a human would.

I am telling you that if you are in a relationship of any kind, where you feel the need to change someone's behavior, or control their freedom, then you do not Love them. Not with a pure heart. Real love has no conditions. Live and let live. If your Limbo starts saying something like, "I love them if.... (Fill in the blank)....", then there is a problem with you and not with them. Imagine that someone would say to you, "I love you, and I would love you even more if you were less stubborn, or less fat, or less opinionated," or whatever you want to put after the "if." Then you don't truly love them. Maybe the correct adjective should be "addicted to them," or infatuated by them, or you are just lonely.

True love accepts completely, has compassion and forgiveness as its two allies. Love is the one feeling that is natural because love is our essence, or even better: We Are Love and Love is Us. One, indivisible. We are born already loving and longing for love. Our dogs and pets show us very easily how they love and want love back. Eventually, due to our or their conditioning, we learn other barriers against love, like distrust, jealousy, or violence. These barriers created by our Limbos, make us so confused about loving. Our mind starts to condition itself that unless certain conditions, changes and accommodations are done by our "Loved" ones, then it will allow us to Love. The truth is that the reason we love our pets so much, is because between them and us, there are (usually) no barriers. I say usually, because there are certain pet owners who will condition their love to a pet also. But speaking of a balanced pet owner, it is easy to see a love flow that is similar to bliss.

The Universe puts this amazing example in front of us. When we ask a balanced owner, but an unbalanced lover, to see and follow the examples given by their pet, they will usually come back with answers and excuses such as: "But they don't understand," "They can't talk," "It's just a dog," or my favorite one, "I don't have sex with my dog, so the love is different." As if purity of Love to another human being should be different because of these factors. Love is Love and Life is Love, and we are Life, period. However, I guess your Limbo, your mind wants facts, explanations, justifications. Nevertheless, Love is a feeling, an essence, and an aroma. You don't explain it; you feel it. Like the one you have with your dog or with your child.

Every dog that has passed through my life, I just loved. I did not need a certain group of words to form into my mind to justify the feeling. I just felt it. There is even a saying that goes something like this, "Please God, let me be the person my Dog thinks I am." Yes pure Love, especially from the dog towards us. "Lobo" seems to have a complete grasp on Love; he expresses it as jovially, loudly and happily as it should be shown. It doesn't matter if I am gone 7 minutes or 7 days. There is no amount of Love that he holds away from me, for a later time. Which is another lesson all on itself. There is no bottom of the barrel, when it comes to Love. Love never ends, so no need to save it for a rainy day, ass a matter of fact, the more Love you give, the more Love you have. It is like a muscle; it gets bigger and better with use. Let Your Dog Out and go on giving love all the time. Never fear Love, if you feel it...express it, give it, receive it, enjoy it, bask in it!.

"Lobo" is 8 years old now, and just because he is 56 human years, making him a grown adult, it does not mean that he stopped enjoying life. He goes at life with full force, 100% no less. Always with joy and loving the moment.

Many people happen to get older, and they feel like they have to put on their "grown up" face, wear "grown up" clothes, behave "grown up," and with all these "grown up" attitudes come the worry, the stress, and the anxiety. As if being grown up meant that we have to stop smiling, playing, enjoying. If I was to tell you just one thing to take from this book, it would be that you should never stop being a child. Never stop playing, or dreaming, or smiling. Always have a sense of wonder for even the most "uneventful" moments from your life.

I put quotations on the word "uneventful", because there is always something happening around us if we take the time to pay attention. If we take the time to explore, like my dogs going on a walk, or like the child in the park. We shall never seize from being in "Awe" about the world.

"Lobo" and all dogs are so "enlightened" that they don't need to go into nature to enjoy the moment. Yet if you feel that city life is so distracting, or stressful, then take the time to go into nature where everything is in harmony. There, enjoy the silence, nature noises and the pure air. Practice quieting your Limbo and being still. Do not hold on to nature as your "escape" from Limbo, or you will find yourself depending on nature to be in peace. The purpose is to find stillness anywhere you go, anywhere you are. After all, wherever you are, is where you are supposed to be.

Observe your pets, they are always in the moment.

Even when I take "Lobo" to the veterinarian, he is in the moment. He is nervous but present. He is not in the past or wishing he was somewhere else. He listens to every noise. He smells all smells. He sees everything. Always here. There is no mind. So being apprehensive about the moment is not wrong. Given the opportunity, he would leave, and then move on to the next fun activity. I have him there. I forced him into the situation. Yet, he remains aware of all of the present activities surrounding the Now. So unless you are forced into a situation like prison, there are only three options for the Now. Enjoy it. Accept it. Or remove yourself from it. Lobo is not enjoying the visit to the Vet. He cannot remove himself from it, so he accepts it. As soon as he leaves the Veterinarian's office, he will be in total enjoyment of the ride in the car. He will not get into the car and wallow about his PAST visit to the veterinarian. That situation is gone forever. The Now has moved on and taken a different form.

You might say, well the reason he is not wallowing is because he can't think, otherwise he would. Bingo! Why should you? Instead, I plead you to see it in a different light. Why not ask yourself, "If my mind is a just a tool, and it does not control me, why don't I shut my mind off and enjoy the new shape that the Now has taken?" Yes, it is that simple. Concentrate and pay attention to the new form of your Now. Never mind the recent or far past situation that your Limbo wants you to re-live and re-live and re-live, so you can go on complaining. "Lobo" and all your pets have mastered it. Let Your INNER Dog Out! Remember that a belief is something that you trust to be true, even when there is no evidence of its existence.

Many people believe in God, the person in Heaven dictating the happenings in this world. No problem, this is not a book about changing your mind. However, many people "believe" themselves stupid, jealous, violent, etc. Though, those same people at times have good ideas, are relaxed and loving. Yet, most people choose to believe the negative trait versus the positive. As you grow up, you had plenty of people, teachers, parents, friends who continued to re-enforce these statements. And Boom! It becomes a belief within you. Though you have evidence of both the positive and the negative trait, you re- enforce the negative, because "you believe it," so now you have to play such role, so you re-enforce it even more. If someone tries to contradict you, you snap. "That's not me!!!" "What do you know...? I know myself!" But ...do you? Really?

Of course, you don't know yourself, but your Limbo will defend this position, because it brings drama, and since you think you are the voice in your brain, subsequently if the voice says so, then it is the gospel. Start slowly to question yourself, about anything that "you believe you are." I know it will take time, but after all, it is worth it.

And by all means, do not fear losing any of your beliefs, your Limbo will fight you. However, you are stronger than that little voice. Dogs have no Limbo, so it is easier to rehabilitate them. Even a dog trained to fight and attack, can be untrained and become a lovely house pet. Why? Because they don't identify with the title of aggressive. It is the same concept for you. Retrain yourself from false beliefs and replace them with loving ones. You are special. We all are.

Nobody will ever walk this Earth and see the world from your angle and through your filters. Ever! That's how unique and special you are. Believe that one.

"Lobo" means wolf in Spanish, when he was born, he had a grayish coat and his ears stood up like a wolf, hence his name. Eventually his coat would turn blonde and his ears would fall, so today the only resemblance to a wolf is his name and his caramel eyes. Nevertheless, his name reminds me of the old Latin saying, "Lupus est homo homini" (Man is a wolf to man). And I would probably add that is all due to the Limbo. The voice in the head hunts its host.

Looking into "Lobito's'" eyes, I can find calmness and stillness, no anger, not even the presence of time, just peace. I know I am looking into the eyes of another species, yet it gives me what I need, Love. However, if I stare into the eyes of any human other than my loved ones, I run the risk of being challenged to a fight; our hearts are not in touch, there is separateness. There is a space that should not exist. If I look into a human's eyes, his mind immediately will categorize me, analyze me, judge me, and measure me. While an animal is only trying to read our energy, friend or foe. And if they already know you then just to show Love.

To me, there is nothing more hypnotic, artistic and soulful, that when my dogs and cat stare at me. I can feel their love and peace, penetrating through the thickest part of my being, until they get at the core. They do it often and intensely, and they get to my heart in every occasion. Their eyes give me all the information I need. There is Love. Respect. I let my dog out every time any of them stares at me. I am a happy man, married to Lilou, but these lines make me reflect on the last time we held each others gaze for more than a few seconds. Honestly, I don't know. Why does staring cause so much discomfort, unless is from our pets? Another lesson learned, even as I write. Learn to be comfortable staring into all beings' eyes. Connect.

"Lobo" might not be "useful" in the eyes of human society. He is just my pet, according to them. Even so, as you can see, he is so much more than that. He could be anyone's master. He is beautiful and that is enough. He is a dog and he is in no way confused about his roll. Any other judgment of usefulness to humans, it is just that of the ego of man. He is not a service dog, an athlete dog, the best trained dog, the best behaved or a companion dog, according to human standards, but it does not matter. He is himself, and he understands that is enough. He doesn't need to prove it to himself or anyone else. Human or animal. Detach from the judgment, opinion or ideal from all others. Be comfortable in your own skin and celebrate your uniqueness, just as "Lobo" celebrates his. Let Your Dog Out.

# CHAPTER 8

# Meditation (Us Versus Pets?)

Us versus animal in Meditation, who wins? I am sure some of you would say, US! We are the superior species. If there is one area where my dogs, and especially my cat, have the technique completely under control and with ZERO effort, it is meditation.

First of all, what is Meditation? Well, there are as many definitions as there are sports. But in general, it would be a practice that involves inner regulation of your thoughts with the purpose of quieting the voice inside the head and realizing that we are the body AND the inner spirit, and that the true answers come from within. In other words, Meditation is looking into your silence and inner space, loving it, turning into oneness, with no desire to put anything in it to fill it. From there, depending on whom you talk to, or what you "googled", variations of all kinds are abundant, yet not wrong. Well, from the get go, all my pets, have a leg up on us. They already lack the voice inside the head, and they act by instinct, and from all texts I have read, instinct is the real voice of the SELF. Our pets, with absolutely no effort, have already met the purpose of Meditation.

Another part of this definition is that it is a "practice." Well, again, our pets are rightly ahead. They do not need to practice IT. They are Masters at it. And since they are Masters of quiet awareness and lack the voice inside the head or what I refer to as Limbo, then I would say that it is fair to say that they are Walking-Meditators, 24/7.

What are we? The best of us, struggle to quiet the Limbo and every now and then we are successful. For others, it is an incredibly hard practice. For yet others, it is a boring practice. And there are even the ones that say it is "impossible" or the ones that say, "I am what I think, why would I want to quiet myself?" I suspect that if you are reading this book, you are not in the last group, most likely you are probably in the first two; you can do it, now and then or you find it to be hard yet you don't give up.

If you are in the third group who can truly say that you mastered it and are always in a place of bliss, then I am honored to know that you are reading the words of a struggling master. Yes, a Master, we all are. We just have to know it and let it come out. Let Your Dog Out, I would say.

Even though I had read so much about the benefits of Meditation, it took me a while until I actually sat down, and consciously tried to quiet my Limbo. Sure, I tried to experiment to see if I would disappear or morph, if I was quiet, but never for more than a few seconds. I am sure that all of the human race at one point or another has been involved in some sort of activity which required them to quiet the mind and to do it at a high level. However, must humans don't even know that they were quiet because the Limbo came back to fill the head almost immediately after such activity ended. Even if you were to tell them that they were quiet, most likely they would deny it or would not believe it. But we will go there later, for now let's go to my experience.

The first time I wanted to meditate, I went into YouTube to watch or listen to different examples of "Guided Meditation" or something similar. Once I found the ones that I thought would match with my vibration and energy, I prepared myself by finding a quiet night with no distractions. Being a novice at conscious quietness, it did help a lot to hear somebody tell me to "observe my breath," "to let my body lie on a cloud," "to imagine a peaceful place," etc. The mystical music and the nature sounds, especially the ocean and or rain, were particularly helpful, probably because I am in Love with water.

Regardless, it was very easy for me to quiet my head following a guided Meditation tape. The first time I meditated, I was well into my spiritual transformation, so I suspect that I had been doing some sort of Meditation while walking or driving or doing some other activity, yet I had not paid attention to the silence. This time I wanted to "know" when I was quiet and when my "Limbo" had a hold of me. So all these guided Meditation recordings were helpful, as long as my heart resonated with it. If you are about to dive into Meditation and start like I did, all I can say is that do whatever resonates with you, let it guide you.

Do not examine the words or think about them, just feel them and let them take you into silence. The ones that might resonate with you might not resonate with me, but is OK, it is not wrong. Your journey is yours and yours only. If someone out there claims to be your teacher or a teacher, and he or she points at a particular technique or author, then he is NOT a teacher, and you will be better off following your instincts. There is a plethora of techniques, books, recordings, rituals, sects and groups that will claim that their way IS the way, or worse, that their way is the ONLY way. Stay clear from those, or follow them, whatever your soul speaks to you, but never because someone else said so. Make it your own truth, or it will be a lie. In other words, if you don't have faith in it, then it is not true....for you. Only for you.

Since I had been reading and listening to so many spiritual Masters, I found it easy to quiet my Limbo and very enjoyable to know when I was completely still, and when my Limbo was trying to control me. By learning to be aware of the activity of my Limbo, I could put it on a leash and by scheduling specific time for resting meditation I could get deep into my inner senses rather than just quieting the dialogue in my head. I also made a point of doing mini-meditations, whether it was for a few seconds or a few minutes throughout my day!

I remember Mr. Eckhart Tolle's recommendation to ask myself when my next thought is going to come, and just continue whatever I was doing and be aware of the time, and the kind of thought that would pop. Previous to learning to quiet my head, I already practiced for a long time the art of positive thinking. I guess if you can't quiet it, might as well say nice things. Now I was at the point of Instead of positive thinking, I was practicing positive being. Silence.

From all the guided Meditation examples that I found on the Internet, my favorites were just plain nature sounds. Again, this all goes with your preferences, rather than a rule. I also found that mystic sounds and new-age instrumental music, could take me there too. However, sometimes, I found that my Limbo had the upper hand, so I would then try to find a Guide who specifically spoke about stress, anxiety, calmness, peace, etc.

During these beginnings, I was listening to Abraham Hicks, whose expertise is the Law of Attraction. I, at no time tried to channel a new job or a new car, for those things have not once been of particular importance to me, but I would try to channel a pleasurable day, an excellent resolution to a challenge. The imagination and the way you channel your desires, have been validated time and time again, yet in my particular way I was searching more for stillness and inner peace, so I never touched hard on the subject. Again, I love Abraham, especially when I need a pep talk, a pick-me-up kind of motivation. And still to this day, I go back to her, time and time again, without much thought about a specific manifestation, but more play and motivation, which after all is what she suggests you do rather than worry about a new car in your garage.

Other days I wanted step by step Meditation, meaning I would listen to a teacher asking you to imagine the beach, the sound from the ocean, the energy pouring out of your body, etc. I guess by being flexible you can touch on any style and use the one that suits your mood, Deepak Chopra filled this method, beautifully. I also found that all of Eckhart Tolle's narrations put me in a meditative state, so whenever another style cannot take me into stillness, I go to him. I then would take a look at my cat, "Orly", and see how aware yet relaxed and still she was and would long to get there.

At the beginning of my Meditation journey, I would find myself motivated and energized, seldom at peace and relaxed. This is my particular journey, so it is perfectly understandable if your process has been different; maybe you never needed specific "Steps," or you might need more. All of the processes are correct, there is no one right way. Your triggers to get into the "No- Mind" state might be different than mine, for example, what relaxes you might energize me or vice versa.

I also found that by scheduling my Meditations normally before I go to bed, relaxes me so much that it eventually puts me to sleep. Most spiritual teachers, Zen Monks, masters and religious figures, will tell you that it is very common to fall sleep. It is an on-going joke to hear teachers say, "Try to quiet your mind without falling asleep." So if this is a side effect of your meditations, you are in a very elite circle.

Now, I look at my dogs and cats and though I know when they are in a meditative state, with their eyes opening every now and then and their ears in radar mode, I also know when they are plainly sleeping. They have no clue on what is going on around them, and they are snoring or out for the count, that you can sneak up on them without a problem. Animals in general sleep a great deal; I guess if our minds didn't keep us awake longer than we want, I suspect that we would sleep a little or a good deal more. Just my guess. So, no worries if you fall asleep also, we all do. Yet try to stay alert. However, sleeping, all on its own, is also a form of meditation. Keep that in mind.

Meditation has so many purposes. Almost everything in life can be done in a meditative state. And without being an expert, I suspect that "almost" is not a necessary word, and EVERYTHING in life can be done in that state. Who knows, maybe I am wrong. If your master or teacher is trying to tell you Meditation has "this" or "that" purpose, probably it is because those are the only times he can go into a meditative state. Of course it is better than nothing, but it is not the "whole enchilada."

The one thing that I found in common in all the meditative states I have tried, is that you have to be in the present moment and realizing one self. You can't call it Meditation if you are in the past, even if your mind is quiet I would call it remembering or even reflecting, but not meditating. Meditating requires you to be "HERE" and "Now." Meditating about the future, I don't think so, because it would require your mind to go into a place and time that has not happened, so to me, even if you are in a quiet mind, I would call it imagining or channeling. So be here and now, be quiet but aware. Be in peace and still, but ready to act accordingly. That is the only way to Meditate.

Let's see some of the most popular Meditation purposes and techniques used by different spiritual teachers. The most common purpose is to quiet the mind. No thoughts, just Now and the vibrations given by your soul. Basically when you do it with this sole purpose, all you are trying to do is to go to your origins. Why? Because before you could think, and the Limbo came along with the thoughts, we were beings in stillness just like the rest of the organisms in this world. Why else? Because when you were born, as infants we still operate in a "No-Mind" state.

Vibration and energy is where we came from. Eventually the body was attached to the vibration and energy and a few years into our infancy we learned to think, to decide, to talk, and along with these capabilities came the Limbo, the voice inside the head. This purpose per se is all you need. It is awesome to just feel the tingling and the life that is within us. Your body loves you for it, because you pay attention to it, and in payment, the body sends you good energy, good health, love and peace. The drawback with this purpose is that it is also the one that is more likely to put you to sleep. So I would recommend that you do it in the seated position.

When your mind is empty, your Limbo gets bored and tries to interrupt you and talk to you about this or that problem, about what else you could be doing instead. When you are able to control the Limbo interruptions, your body gets light, your mind is clear, and you feel peace. I have seen this bright light surrounding my body. I have never been close to death, or died and came back, so I don't know how that would feel, but according to the many people that have been there, it is a similar place. If it is, I can see why many do not want to come back from that ecstasy. So if this is your simple way of Meditation and you can stay awake, by all means continue to harvest this way of being.

By the way this is where our dogs are at all times, whether they are awake and active, or just before they fall asleep. Empty mind, peaceful body. Nothing else is needed. In other words, you die without dying. This is the closest you will ever feel to being one with the Universe, including those whose bodies have dissolved. I should stop right here, this all you need. Be here, be one, be all, be everywhere and anywhere at the same time.

If you have ever truly emptied your mind, you found yourself in the present moment and having a presence, where no problems or judgments exist. In other words, total bliss and mindfulness. This is what Buddhists call "Vapasana" and is done naturally by all animals. If you have a pet, and he comes to your lap, turn your TV off, be silent and share Vapasana with them. Eventually, both of you will fall asleep. Let it be. It is what it is. I can assure you that even the nap will be one of your most peaceful ever. Let Your Dog Out.

Another type of Meditation is the one that you practice while seated in a Lotus position or modified Lotus. During this meditation, you repeat a mantra, such as "ohmmmm" "ohmmmm" or "rammm", "rammm" or any sound that you choose, as long as this is what keeps the Limbo from creeping in to give you a thought. This style of meditation has worked for me, especially when I combine it with Yoga or my daily exercise. Since my body was being put through a rigorous demand and concentration, the quietness was necessary to perform at a high level. It seems that my mind wants to talk to me right after I finish. So I have to distract it, educate it if you will. Tell my Limbo that I am boss, and I don't want it coming in just yet. For that I need to distract it.

Our dogs do not use this or follow any technique, but we humans need them once in a while, until vapasana becomes our natural, everyday state. I use it only for a few minutes and try to go into just stillness and silence as soon as possible. I understand some self-proclaimed gurus have boasted the fact they are able to leave their body. To me that indicates they are still ruled by Limbo or ego, because they, one, "Claim" to leave their bodies and two, they want their students to seek this state. Is it possible? I do not know. I have never been there, where I leave my body. If that is your goal, follow your goal, but know that you are not in the Now anymore. Why? Because you have set a goal, and goals always operate in future. If you stumble into an out of body experience, then is pure; but setting a goal occupies the future.

Another type of Meditation is Kundalini. I have never practiced it and probably never will. Just to know that a spiritual "technique" has a potential for side effects (Kundalini Syndrome) is enough for me to leave it in peace. However, you might happen to be reading this book, and someone told you that this technique would help you. In simple words, it involves concentration into your breath flow through each energy center (Chakra) and always moving upward. The so called syndrome is the potentiality to be stuck in a certain level or chakra, and not be able to get out. In that case the remedy would be worse than the ailment. But please do not listen to me, follow your own path. Experience what ever comes in vibrational match with you.

The "Chi," or circulation of energy Meditation, centers in the three spots of Tao Meditation. Stomach, Chest and Forehead. This is another very complex meditation that requires practice rather than going back to your original nature. All methods try to get you to your original nature, but through steps rather than acceptance of what is during your practice. Again, my argument is that no other being would need to follow a technique. However, so many people need the structure of a technique in order to get into their inner self. If you need it, use it.

The "Guided Visualization" method, I do use, especially in slow moments at work or when I am driving, or even before I go to sleep. This is usually done by listening to a recording asking you to imagine yourself lying in a cotton field or on the sandy beach, listening to the waves. I use this passive meditation when I cannot Let My Dog Out, and just be quiet within. So instead of letting my Limbo control what goes in it, I supplant it with beautiful talks from any guru, which puts me in peace, especially Eckhart Tolle, Deepak Chopra or Osho. Even so, sometimes your mind does not even want you to listen to these beautiful talks; then I go to plan "B." I go to authors that are more in the level of form yet beautiful, such as Dr. Dyer, Ms. Hay, Abraham or Don Miguel Ruiz. They are still in the level of thought, but beautiful thoughts, nevertheless. Positive thinking is ALWAYS better than useless, negative or judgmental thoughts. Do not follow one technique or one way. There is not "A Way." Just find your peace, any way you can.

Another type of Meditation that I would like to learn about but do not know very well, is the "Heart Rhythm" meditation. This meditation is similar to the Mindfulness Meditation, which concentrates in the breath, and centers its energy into the heart and then identifies with it. Someday I will look more into it, but I suspect that every time you are guided by Love you are basically practicing this meditation. And our dogs and pets are always identified with the heart because they have so much love to give.

I can already circulate energy to different parts of my body, but how to use our energy in service of my heart, sounds blissful in theory, but are we already doing that? I believe we are.

One of my all time favorite forms of meditation its The Laughing Meditation, not so much where you get together and just laugh and laugh, though it quiets the mind; I am mostly referring at never ever loosing your sense of humor, specially about yourself. My dogs are always in joy and seemed to be laughing and enjoying what ever present moment they are in. Laugh often, laugh loud, laugh hard.

As you can see there are several "methods" of doing meditation, yet I always go back to the fact that meditation is "being" not "doing." My dogs are not doing their state of peace; they are being it. My dogs don't have to try doing anything they just ARE. Anything you ever 'do' in life, you have to 'BE' first. No being, no doing. You have to exist before you can take any action.

So by default your being is always more important than any action you take. Go ahead and make lots of money but do not forget who you are, and I can assure you, you are not your possessions, nor your achievements.

Remember always not to be hard on yourself. Enjoy your journey. Yes, thoughts and Limbo will creep inside, but you don't have to follow those thoughts, just observe them. Laugh at them. Yes, your Limbo will find that meditation is boring; pay no attention to it. Stay centered. Stay here. Stay Now. Slowly, you will find that your peaceful state of being is more important than any idea or thought trying to creep in.

As you can see, meditating can be as simple as quieting your mind and being present, or it can go into actual techniques with different purposes. Go where your heart wants to go. Yes, it is that simple. I am sure there are other methods that I am not even aware of. Nevertheless, follow your bliss. The heart never lies. What keep animals alive are their hearts, their instincts, and their gut feelings. It will keep you living too. No lie.

Please do not get frustrated by outside noises, thoughts, alarms, or any circumstance that "disturb" you. Anything that disturbs you is a judgment; the situation is what it is. Let it go, or use it as the mantra needed to quiet your mind. Become a friend of the so-called disturbance, and it will cease to be a disturbance, and it will become a hook into mindfulness. When you become a friend of your distractions, whether for Meditation or sleep, they automatically disappear. What keeps you awake is not the noise but rather, your thoughts about them. Stay in your Meditation, rather than find an excuse not to do it. If you Meditate as one with it, as your own being, rather than something you are doing, then it will listen to you and allow you in.

Another question that I have heard many times is: Where should I Meditate? Some people insist in creating their "special" place or going to a particular teacher or temple. The Western world has created a marketing machine around the spiritual movement. You have Yoga clothes, Yoga centers, Buddhist beads, Meditation TV by enrollment. There are businesses that are not even close to being spiritual using the word Tao, Buddha, Ohm, Karma, Namaste, etc. Or you have to go to a "certification" process to be enlightened, as if that was possible! You can find spiritual guide courses or life coach training, really? You have jewelry with Buddhist forms, such as the tree of life, the ohm, Buddha, etc. that make you feel cool. But do they? What you wear or how many certificates you have, or how many techniques you were certified in, DO NOT make you an enlightened person.

This is the one that not even Hollywood stars or rich people can buy. You ARE or you are not. So many people "act" spiritual. They wear the "spiritual" clothes. They talk the "spiritual" lingo or go to Yoga. And suddenly they feel "more" spiritual than the "others." Who are the others? The ones that do not wear the clothes or speak the lingo, or drink coffee, drink alcohol, or eat meat!!! "Oh no!!! You cannot be enlightened. You do all those nasty things. What kind of course have you taken anyway?"

All that is Limbo talk, Ego talk...but yet the Western world will recognize those who play the role. Profit seems to be the aim, rather than the spiritual well-being of another. I am not saying that payment should not come to you if you perform a service. However, the service should be the aim, not the profit.

Your level of consciousness is more important than your appearance or your certificates. So many people feel more spiritual than others because they "walk the talk" and live the roll in the level of form rather than the humble way of just being. Others feel they are more spiritual because they have a meditating space. By all means enjoy the beauty of the clothes and the jewelry, get all the certificates that you want, read all the books, but know that none of them get you into enlightenment. I practice Yoga myself, but so does your cat and dog when they stretch! I buy some of the cool Buddhist jewelry, and clothes, but just because I like them. I feel just as in harmony wearing a police uniform and a gun as I do wearing cowboy boots or nightclub clothing. Yes, I go dancing too! Awesome form of meditation.

My dogs are in harmony in their fur, why shouldn't you be? My dog does not go to a meditation center, but I am not saying you shouldn't. All I am saying is that you have to realize all this "form" does not make you spiritual. At their best, they point you towards IT. The room for your Meditation is INSIDE you. To find your SELF, you don't need a particular place, situation, person or possession. You are either enlightened or you are not. No certificate is needed either, and those who are awakened will show you the doors but let you choose which ones to walk through.

I remember going on a cruise where I was supposed to give a meditative talk. For whatever reason, it was not scheduled, yet a couple of ladies were hoping that I showed up. They started doing a form of channeling to let go of physical pain, which one of them was suffering due to an accident. When they saw me, they said, "We were waiting for you, but noticed that it was not scheduled. So I started doing some channeling with her" she then asked me what kind of technique I used. I said, "Nothing really, just the moment." Her eyes rolled into her head and looked at me while saying "if you don't have any certificates or formal training, how can you help her?". Certificates and degrees influenced her. I did not "look" like an enlightened person, I was not wearing "the clothes" of an enlightened person. I did not "walk the talk" of an enlightened person, and I did not have the training of an "enlightened" one. I have tattoos! All forms of ego trips. The western world is just like that.

Even so, this is very typical of the Western world. You are what you "look" like and what you can show that you studied. Do not fall into that box. Your dogs, after all, can go in front of a prince and remain in stillness. So can you. Just as my dogs can deal with any human, regardless of title, the same, so should you. Enlightenment is not found in time, in a situation, a person, a book or a certificate. It is found in the here and now, by anyone at anytime. Appearances, clothes, looks, certificates, money, friends, influence, political affiliation, nationality, color, race, gender, sexual orientation, fame; in short NOTHING plays a role into enlightenment.

My wife "Lilou" has a beautiful black cat named "Orly", whom I observe from time to time, as the best example of how to be in perfect meditation. She can be still, yet aware. At peace, yet alert. She does not require a particular place, or garments, or a method. Meditation and she are one. She is consistently moving her ears like radar, even when her eyes are closed or semi-closed, Other times she seems to be lost into a spot on the wall, just staring. She can be in the same position for a long time.

My exercise consists of trying to match "Orly". I always loose, but someday-now I will match her..... When it comes to Meditation, a cat is the perfect role model. They do not need a particular technique. Rely on your favorite technique, ritual or steps, until you realize that none are needed. Do not stop your methods of Meditation, even if I tell you so. Believe no one. Not even your favorite Spiritual Teacher. Only stop using props when you are ready. It is your journey.

Realize that no steps are needed to become enlightened, only doors. Walk through them as your instinct tells you. And realize that your best teachers will point at the doors, but never ever will make you go through them.

A student recently asked me if she could call me her Spiritual Master. As often as I use the word Master, for my dogs, cat and spiritual authors, understand that we are all students and teachers at the same time. You are your own Master. You and only you can cross through any door pointed out by a teacher. It is your decision, at any given time, what makes you remain in suffering or realize the end of suffering. As long as your mind is controlled by Limbo, you will not believe that you are your own Master. When you enter the timeless Now, you will regain control over your mind and the Self.

If Religion is your path in order to get answers, follow your bliss, reach into yourself to find the God within. No way of enlightenment or Meditation is a wrong way. As you find your Inner God, you will find that outer situations and attitudes will manifest to reflect your inner peace. Ultimately no outer situation, thing, event or person will be able to disturb your inner peace. Once you find yourself in the state of No-Mind, you will have become one with Meditation. Essentially you will become a "Walking Meditator," and the use of your mind will take a step aside into the toolbox.

Nevertheless, always be aware that the Limbo will fight you. It will try to con you into believing that all "this" spiritualism is just 'mambo-jumbo', it's boring. It's dangerous; it's deadly. Most spiritual teachers experience a big fall, prior to enlightenment. So don't despair, it is the Limbo putting up a final battle before extinction. It might show up in the form of an illness, loss of loved ones, loss of property, loss of status. You never know how it will show up. But whatever it is, it will be accompanied of a banner that says "Can you handle it?".

Am I enlightened or in Meditation at all times, as my dogs, cat or the Dalai Lama or Eckhart Tolle appear to be? No, is my answer. I am tested by life, time and time again. My Limbo comes ahead of me on many occasions, and those are my best teachers. I know then that I still have work to do. Don't despair for your lost battles; welcome them. But most important, learn from them.

Heaven and Hell reside within you, and it is the one that you get more identified with, that will reflect your inner and outer world. The closer you come into knowing faithfully that your quiet stillness is your true self, the sooner you will be One with life.

My dogs and all living beings, except humans, have it from birth and never lose it, even those pets that live within a dysfunctional home. Reach IN, not out. Let Your Dog Out!

Finally, I leave this topic with a method that I discovered recently through social media. This method is aimed at allowing you to fall asleep in nearly one minute. It is called "The 4-7-8 Breath". It basically a breathing technique that helps you lower your blood pressure, therefore relaxing you and eventually putting you to sleep. You breath in for four seconds, hold your breath for seven seconds and breath out for eight. Since I started using it I can go to sleep so much faster and deeper. But I have taken the practice a little bit further, whenever I feel a bit nervous, anxious or upset. Yes, I still experience all those emotions, I use it to calm me down. I have included this technique in this chapter because to me is a form of meditation for two reasons; one, because you keep count of you seconds, therefore emptying your mind of other useless thoughts; and two, because sleep Per Se, is a form of meditation all by itself. I love this technique, though I know my dogs can't count nor they monitor their breath. How ever this method allows me to Let My Dog Out.

# CHAPTER 9

# Master Orly the Cat!

Before I go into "Letting your Cat Out," I will shortly say that after I lived with "Tash" and then moved back into my condo, I found myself with four of the five dog masters. I taught them to walk without a leash, and just to follow my commands. Though not even close to what Cesar Millan can do, it worked in our relationship. As time went on, and Olivia and I were getting closer to one last try at our relationship, I found that my search for more than just being positive was knocking at my door. I bought *A New Earth* and picked up *The Power of Now* once again.

This time Mr. Tolle made all the sense in the world, his words that had put me to sleep years before, were more alive than ever. I heard every YouTube message by him that I could get my hands on. The light was flickering in the distance, but this time I knew the secret.... the light is here, now, in the present moment and not in a future goal. All of a sudden, all seemed very simple you might say. I was awakened "in short bursts," you may call it. The real secret was revealed to me.

So by the time Olivia and I gave it one last last shot, I had tasted enlightened moments. I was serious that this was my last try, regardless of how we would end up. Well, it was our last try. One night she said goodbye forever. Valid reasons or not, we were finished. A few months later, I would meet "Lilou".

When I met my wife and visited her in France, I also met "Orly" the cat. She is a skinny black, female, cat, with a white spot on her chest. She has medium-length hair, which she sheds like it is going out of style. A co-worker of my wife found her roaming around the Orly airport in the parking lot in the outskirts of Paris, France. Hence her name. She is not as much of a character as some of the cat videos I have seen, but she is a cat alright.

This is my very first time having the privilege of cohabiting with one, and though I am very allergic to cat dandruff, I can learn from her just by observing. She only trusts my wife and she is always aware of the location of your feet if you are walking near her. I have a suspicion that a male probably kicked her in the past. I don't know cat psychology, but there is definitely a calmed but aware carefulness about my feet. She was also possibly the only cat in her past home because she is very aggressive towards other cats. This also suggests that she was probably taken from her mom at a very early age, since she only demonstrates active aggression against other felines. On the other hand, she is tolerant of the dogs, as long as they are not too close to her space, which sometimes is a bigger space than my dogs calculate, and they have to run away from her.

Obviously, my dogs respect her, and possibly have a little fear of her. In other words, they avoid her as much as possible, even with their eyes. It is so funny to see them avoiding eye-to-eye contact, as if that would make them invisible to "Orly"! Nevertheless, once in a while, a paw on their romp for invading this cat's space surprises them.

It has been about four years now that "Orly" is our roommate. Unlike my dogs, who show me that I am the Alpha male of their pack and respect me, "Orly" is another story all together. She loves "Lilou" but on her own terms. She is more like the roommate you always wanted. She respects your privacy, yet asks for the same back; however, she is willing to be there for you as long as it doesn't conflict with her schedule.

This was possibly the best lesson that I learned, right from the beginning. Right away, I noticed that she was not like a dog in terms of being right next to you regardless of what you are doing. No, she comes to you, only when she wants and in her own time. Independence! Yes, that is the lesson. Learn to be happy in your own skin, and in your own company. A cat does.

Though they understand that we are all one, and that they eventually need love and affection, food and shelter, they do not cling to you. Space and respect. Even what some might call, selfishness. However, this kind of selfishness is healthy. Care for your needs, groom yourself, have your beauty sleep, play, meditate; then and only then go check on your loved ones. This is not to be taken literally, for you are not a cat. But rather as the spiritual message that it represents. The beauty of never feeling lonely when you are alone. This lesson I had to learn on my own, a few years before I met "Lilou" and "Orly", but I am sure I would have sped up the learning if I had had a cat to watch and learn from.

Another lesson that I fell in love with was her gift of awareness at all times. It is very, very difficult to surprise a cat. Though it is possible, it is never because they lacked awareness. It is just because you surprised them while in actual deep sleep or while being attentive to another subject, there is no other reason. It is so beautiful to watch her, apparently resting on top of her favorite couch, and see her ears move around like a radar, listening for everything around. Every once in a while her eyes lazily open, just to make sure that the noise has no potential danger. They can sit in stillness and awareness for the longest time. Just to see them gives you the basis of meditation. Quiet awareness. No-Mind. Stillness and completely in the present moment. Perfect Zen master.

If you can imitate your cat when meditating, you are already a Master. If you can carry a quiet awareness into your everyday actions, you can consider yourself a graduate of cat-school. Which is a very high honor.

Orly has been the quiet teacher. I wish to be. While my dogs are full of energy and happiness, she is cool and collected. She is always sure of herself, confident, and royal. Your thoughts and judgments are of no concern to her. She feels pretty, so she is pretty. I have seen this trait in some women. And it is so attractive to see confidence with no arrogance. That is "Orly". If she was human, nobody would say that she is arrogant, she just knows what she wants and when. Other than that, she can walk into any room and take over the energy of it.

As humans, we are our own worst judges. Since I started my journey, I made a point of raising my eyesight from the ground to eye level. I try to walk deliberately and be sure of my steps. I do not hurry, unless I am late. I don't pretend to act with superiority, but for sure I do not feel inferior to anyone. We are all unique beings, and nobody will ever be you again. We are all special. "Orly" knows it and is not shy to show it. Watch your thoughts about yourself; if you must use your mind, make sure is in a loving manner.

Have you ever seen your cat in full Meditation and then they open their eyes wide and stare at the apparently empty wall? And as they watch intently, sometimes they swab at the empty air? I am no cat behavior expert at all. Even so, this book is not about that. The message to me is that occasionally, we are confronted by our own imagination going wild, and it is necessary to watch the feeling that we caused ourselves. Let it pass through and wipe it off of your mind.

I am not sure if "Orly" is watching something I just cannot see, or if she is just releasing bad energy out. However, I see the benefit in acting as she does, when worries, tension, stress or any bad vibe is running through us. I can tell the difference when "Orly" is probably seeing an insect move, because she gets ready to hunt, and sometimes does. No, I am talking about when she just stares and gently moves her paw into the air. Some mystics believe that cats can see energy moving around. If that is true, then it would make sense how they wave it off so it won't enter them.

I remember going out for a drink with "Tina" years ago, and in the group was a friend of hers by the name of "Marc Anthony" (not the singer), and he had this trick or whatever you want to call it. He would ask you to hold your arms out, close your fists, and then he would lower your energy, without touching you. He would ask you to resist him trying to lower your arms. With little or no effort, he could do it. He then would repeat the experiment, but this time he would raise your energy, again without touching you, by waving and lifting the air around your body in an upward motion. I then would resist and have much more power to avoid him lowering my arms. True story.

Just because we don't see the aura of energy that we all walk around with, it does not mean it does not exist. So I tend to believe that "Orly" avoids a lot of bad energy by simply pawing at it and moving it along. It would explain why they are cool and collected most of the time. Something to think about.

"Orly" knows our home from one end to another, so do the dogs. They know exactly when something new has been put somewhere, or when something has been changed of its location. The dogs usually go sniff it, examine it, and I am sure some dogs mark it as theirs, not my dogs. But they do observe it, sniff it and learn from it. "Orly", on the other hand, will rub her body past it after first inspecting it. I guess she is putting her dandruff on the item as a way of claiming it too. However, that is not where I am going with this message.

Our pets know everything about the house and will inspect it every so often to make sure nothing is out of the ordinary. Do you even pay attention to your domain? Be it your home, your work route, your gym route, etc.? By domain, I speak of the most usual places and routes you take. Do you really know when something changes? Or are you like most people, who live so immersed in their head, that something important or out of the norm could be right in front of you and you would not even notice?

By being a policeman, I can tell you that 99% of the people are so concentrated or distracted with their thoughts, that it is the reason why they become victims of crimes. Criminals are always looking for opportunities, and there are plenty out there. Are you a sheep? Are you a sheepdog? Or are you the wolf? Our pets really know what is going on in their domain at all times. The same can be said in the spiritual realm; watch your thoughts!

The sheep in the spiritual sense would be the negative, judgmental, living in the head, victim.... victim of the Limbo. Who is the Limbo? The wolf...always watching how to get you in its jaws. Be the sheepdog, guard your thoughts and keep the Limbo at bay. Do not go with the motions, both in the world of form and in your soul. In the world of form, you will miss the dangers, but most important you will miss the beauty of the present moment. Even if you drive the same route daily, if you pay attention, you will notice that some things have changed, because ultimately, nothing ever stays the same.

In your spiritual self, you start by guarding your thoughts and eventually become a silent, present soul, who enjoys and smiles at the changes in the world. The more often you go within, the more you will see what is happening inside of you, and the body loves the attention too. Healing also happens when you go within as often as possible and nurse yourself. Pay attention to both your inner and your outer world as often as possible.

"Orly" is very independent, so is "Trece", but not quite as much as the cat. "Orly" will entertain herself, nurse herself, groom herself, play alone, hunt alone, explore on her own while never feeling lonely. If she needs company, she will reach out to "Lilou", then go back doing her own thing. Being alone is not equal to being lonely. Lonely is feeling as if the world or the Universe would owe you something. Loneliness is telling the Universe that your situation ought to be different and you need to be in somebody's company.

I remember when I used to get lonely. I would wish for an imaginary girlfriend who would make my life better, then cry because she did not exist. I would feel sorry for myself for not having friends or things to do with people. Lonely left on its own the moment I found that 'I' am Love. Automatically! No effort. It is very clear that when you don't love yourself, all the nasty emotions are present. Jealousy, loneliness, shyness, anger, or negativity. Gone! Poof!

Let me tell you something, you cannot fool your inner self. If you are still experiencing some of those emotions there is work to be done. Embrace the chance that your body gives you as a perfect teacher, and work on it. No need to work on the emotion, just find your Self Love. Realize that YOU ARE LOVE. Even so, while that happens, learn from your body and your emotions.

"Lilou" does not own "Orly"; she only cares for her. "Orly", and I suspect every cat for that matter, have no owners. They will gladly accept that you clean their box, that you refill their water jug and you feed them. Apart from that, they do as they please and ARE as they are. If anything, they own you. "Orly" does not accept other cats. I suspect because she does not want to share her "Queendom" (is that a word?). She probably would have to battle for head of the household with another cat.

Humans and dogs, well, we are easy to manage. All kidding aside, "Orly" gives us another good lesson in behavior. There is no relationship, be it romantic, friendly or working that should make you feel like they own you or vice versa. If you are in a relationship where your partner calls you "mine," you may want to analyze if it is just a common use of words, like "my wife," "my love." However, if the person you are with uses the "my" or "mine" in the literal way, as a possession or property, you may want to see why you are willing to accept that title. Same if you feel like you own somebody else. You do not own your dog, nor your cat, nor your husband, or your wife, your friends, or even your car.

This is probably one of the first lessons that we are taught as children. This is "your name," "my toy," "my puppy," etc. Since a very early age, humans are taught the importance (not really) of ownership, and together with that comes the lesson of protecting, defending, directing and even destroying "your property" as you see fit. Even some laws give the husband the "wife rights," other laws call pets "property." These phenomena go back as far as there was a thinking mind within the human. Right of ownership came with the Limbo. If you believe by now that you are not the voice inside the head, by the result you should understand that you own NOTHING.

Wars have been fought to defend "my family name," "my religion," "my country," "my race," or, "my borders." Wherever you go you can come across examples of arguments, fights, disagreements, failed relationships, wars, all in the name of "my so and so, and you have disrespected it".

"Orly", and really all animals own nothing. They protect their territory not as a duty to defend what is "theirs," but just as an instinct to preserve their lives and their instinct to extend their lineage. If my cat is very protective of her favorite window, she can be taught that there is no threat in sharing. Once the lesson is learned, "she does not own the window." Same with my dogs. If he protects the backyard and I introduce the feeling that is OK for anybody to come to it, the dog will accept it. My dogs love everyone, so I am sure they would accept a stranger in my backyard more easily than I would. For them it is a decision whether it is a threat or not, not about owning the property. Same I could say about their favorite toy. Yes, they will protect it, if they are using it, but they will allow another of my dogs to play with it whenever they want. There is no sense of "mine." Even in the pack no one owns the other; they love the other.

Even when "Chubis" was following "Trece" everywhere she went, when he wanted to mate; it did not mean that he felt entitled to her. He just wanted her sexually, and she had to accept him to be a mating ritual. Nowhere was a sense that "Chubis" had the right to use "his" girlfriend, whenever he wanted. This is a very difficult lesson to pass on to people. Even very spiritual persons will lose their wits or temper when "their" possession is threatened. As I walked through my journey into enlightenment, I could let go more and more of the sense of ownership. My wife has to do nothing just because she is "my" wife. She goes and comes as she pleases, and this was very difficult for her to understand at first. Though she welcomed the freedom, her Limbo associated a relationship to rules and limits.

I go back to "Orly", because her relationship with "Lilou" is based on respect and Love. Self Love first. As you know, it is very difficult to set rules and limits for a cat. They obey their own rules and hope that you can live with them. There is never a question in her head, "Let me see what "Lilou" thinks about what I am doing." A healthy relationship should be based in trust, Love and freedom. Humans tend to give fewer rules to their pets, and in the same breath they mutter that they wish they could find a human to love as their pets love them. Well, it starts with no ownership and no rules. Let your friends and partners be exactly who they want to be.

"Orly" is curious, that is her nature. She wants to know "what is going on".... always. The closer, or on top of the action, the better. On top of you, blocking your view sounds logical to her. Once she gets serious about wanting to be there, well, she is there, and it's impossible to continue doing what you were doing. Curiosity is a wonderful thing, to have a sense of wonder for everything that we see. It's a lost art that humans had at one point during childhood. To have curiosity is to be interested in the world in front of us, and to remain in the present moment. If you are curious like a cat, you are interested in whatever is happening in front of you. It is impossible to be, mentally, somewhere else if the subject of our curiosity is right in front of us. You are there and no where else.

Unfortunately as we get older, we are less curious and interested in the mundane, everyday, simple, wonderful things in life. Humans become adults, and they are curious about the wrong things. Humans are curious about misery, gossip, and drama.

When we were children, just like a cat, a box became a castle. A flower, an awesome aroma. The grass was our playground. Little ladybugs would entertain us forever just by walking on our hand. Watching a worm inch its way from one spot to another was mesmerizing. Then the Limbo happened. Ego took over and started to talk more and more and more. Some people became so identified with the voice, that it became their identity. Curiosity for life became a "waste of time." Why? The happiest most relaxing days of my life were my childhood. Even when the voice came, I could enjoy hours sitting on the branch of a tall tree. Or playing fut-bol with my mates on the street, or going to the nearby mountains, treasure hunting. Curiosity. Wonderful to have a sense of wonder about life.

"Orly" sets the example for curiosity. And I can't help but smile, because my inner self remembers, and it knows that curiosity is a form of meditation. Be curious again; rediscover the wonder of our simple life. Namaste.

"Orly", as well as all cats, is athletic. Oh what a wonderful sight to see her leap with such grace, precision and beauty. How many times I wish to be a cat. They are so flexible also. No yoga expert will come as close as that, ever. But it is not about becoming a cat, but to learn the lesson from the cat. In terms of the body, it teaches us to exercise it, to flex it, to stretch it, and make it a lifestyle. I try, even in my early 50s. I don't see myself slowing down anytime soon. It is a lifestyle for me just as it is for "Orly". Nevertheless, the lesson is deeper than that; as important as it is to care for the temple, it is the lesson of flexibility of mind that is more important. To be able to bend and not break is a beautiful lesson. In life, we always will come face to face against challenges and inevitable changes. Every situation, event, person or thing has a cycle, and within that cycle, challenges and changes happen. No exception. From that premise, you know that in many situations you have to go through by bending, adapting, morphing and sometimes changing with the situation at hand. If you learn to bend and not to resist or fight, then half the battle is won. To bend does not mean that you allow every situation to mold you, no, to bend it means that you go with the flow like water, yet you keep your essence. To bend does not mean to become the challenge, but like the strong wind and the palm tree, you go with the flow of the wind, never resist it, then you come back stronger. Flexibility of mind means that you are open to all possibilities without judgment. All ideas and opinions are valid; the gain or the loss of material things is accepted with the same humility. The anger of a person is understood and observed, but never fought. Just to be flexible of body and mind will allow you to be in radical acceptance of the present moment, knowing that your comeback will be stronger. Regardless of how desperate and dark your situation is, if you are flexible on the face of the challenge, it will allow you the space necessary to be at peace while in it. Nothing ever remains the same; everything changes and morphs, both the good and the bad. So be flexible.

"Orly" can see in the dark. She can move through darkness as if it was a sunny, clear morning for our eyes. Yes, she can maneuver around objects with precision and control. To her, darkness is a friend because as a cat grows, he or she learns that other prey cannot see as well, making darkness an ally rather than a foe. I always loved the dark. I was mildly afraid of it, but never terrified. And I am talking strictly about light versus no light. However, for many years I carried a heavy, thick darkness within me. My Limbo. Yes, the voice inside your head loves darkness, and it makes you fear it. As I told you in my story, I carried the darkness of jealousy, anger, possessiveness, distrust, no self-confidence, etc. All those emotions come from darkness, and the more I "hated" being that way, the more I had occasions to display those emotions. Not only because it is the law of energy to attract that what you are, but also because I was resisting it. "That which you resist, persists." It wasn't until I learned to embrace my darkness through self-love that those emotions started to dissipate due to the light I was shining on it. Whatever your darkness is at this moment, the first thing you need to do is to embrace it and become a friend of it. Notice that I did not say to become it. Acceptance of the situation does not mean that you don't act on it. It only means that you surrender to it and from that space you act. No attachment, no judgment. The darkness can be a wonderful teacher. However, in order to be a student of the darkness, you have to let go of any fear or attachment to it. In other words, so many people find themselves deep into darkness of some kind, be it addiction, illness, their mental state, etc. that their first reaction toward it is fear. Then the next step they take is to fight it, and eventually when they see that all is lost, they attach to it. They become it. Those are the people that as soon as you meet them, they say, "I am a cancer survivor" or "I am very ill," or "I like my drink," or "I am jealous, and I can't change that." Those people probably already went through the fear and the fight, and now "if you can beat them, join them" syndrome. But I am quite certain that they never tried to embrace, accept and be friends with "such" darkness. Because once you do, you become a cat in the dark. One with the darkness. And eventually you are the light, and where is light there is no darkness. A cat does not understand what darkness is since they see as clear as they see during the day. That is the place where you want to go. The place where you say, "Darkness? What darkness?" We all know what our dark spots are. We don't need a spiritual teacher to point them out. You just have to go within, find them and instead of confronting them, you comfort and befriend them. Make your change from there. Let Your Cat Out!

Just recently, while I was finishing this chapter, "Orly" decided to take a walk outdoors and explore our neighborhood. She is an inside cat, so naturally we were worried how she would fend for herself, even if she could survive one night. After the 4th night of her departure, and after looking all over the surroundings, we thought that she was gone for good. We did not give up and placed fliers on every corner and went to the animal shelter to make sure Animal Control hadn't picked her up. We had no luck finding her, dead or alive. On the eve of the 7th day, I went outside to walk the dogs. I heard the sound of her little bell, but it was so dark that I could not see her. I stood there blocking the access to the open street and waited. "Orly" then ran towards the driveway of our house and just crouched there. I yelled, from my blocking position, to get "Lilou" to come out. After many attempts, "Lilou" finally came out and grabbed "Orly". She was gone almost 7 days and she had come back.

I know that this is not uncommon, to see cats come back after several days, but I also knew that there was a message to learn from it. This was not the first time that "Orly" had gone out, but this was the longest outing. Prior to her last escape, she had been acting a little odd. She was shedding chunks of hair, appeared stressed, and she was making weird callings. "Orly" is fixed, so I knew it had nothing to do with being in heat, but I have no idea why it was so important for her to go back out, and probably I will never know.

Nevertheless, I could relate to her stress while in a loving relationship. I had several relationships in the past where I was the person holding on too tight, and in others, the girl was making me feel like I could not breathe. I told "Lilou" my opinion. I told her that she was holding on too tight to the fact that she did not want her cat to go out, and this kind of love was making "Orly" feel the need for freedom. My words exactly were "You are loving "Orly" to death," and I meant it literally. I explained that it was impossible to hold any relationship so tight that the other feels like life is asphyxiating. I told my wife that in this and in all relationships, she needed to relax and let the other be who they are. Let them go and if they come back, their love was yours, but if they don't is because they are better being free.

Either way is a winning situation. It might not feel like a winning situation to you if the other does not want to be with you because your Limbo is trying to tell you that "you are the best for them," or that "without them, there is no life." But all these messages from the voices in your head are all lies. You cannot hold on to somebody so tight that his or her only thought is to leave and be free. That is the by-product of possessiveness and jealousy. Instead hold on to your relationships, like water. With care and softness, because the moment you squeeze water, it slips out of your hand.

To this day, "Orly" has not tried to get out again, but it is very possible that she will. Either way is fine, because whatever is her instinct, it will be the correct decision for her, and by default the precise decision for the rest of us. I can hear your mind turning and saying, "Oh yeah? Then why do you walk your dogs with a leash then?" "Trece" walks without one, and in the past "Morris" and "Lobo" did also, but they have not learned to be well-behaved pedestrians, and they used to cross the street without looking, hence the leashes.

However, I can leave the door open on a nice day, and though they could go and run away if they wanted, they never do. I play as little interference in their lives as possible. I hope that they will stay forever, but it is not a guarantee. Nevertheless, they are free as any domesticated pet can be. I allow them to Let Their Dog Out!

# CHAPTER 10

# Doggie Love VS Human Love

I have been observing my dogs and my cat on the issue of love. Yes, I know how everyone says that dogs give you unconditional love and they put you ahead of their needs. But is it? Well, I have been watching them, and I have seen how Love begins with the Self first. I especially wanted to check this issue, not only because the common misconception is that dogs will put you first, and this I believed would go against the spiritual teaching that wants you to Love yourself first. What better way to see Love than to see a Mother's love?

When "Trece" became a mother of "Lobo" and two other puppies, I noticed that though she loved her pups, she took care of herself first. She ate well and before feeding the pups, she cleaned herself before cleaning the babies. All this was done by instinct. There was no voice inside her head to say, "Help your babies first, or you are a bad mother." No, her instinct would rather say, "You cannot care for others unless you care for yourself first." Even so, this was not the only instance where I saw that their survival and self-love were first, and from those premises, they will give unconditional love.

However, before you can love yourself first and foremost, you have to quiet the Limbo voice. Otherwise, it will try to make you feel guilty, or it will tell you to only love yourself. Both extremes are not going to take you to peace. Balance is in the center. However, if you start with self-love, you will be able to give away the same amount of love you have for yourself. I grew up without ever having a pet until my adult life. Examples of true love were not in front of me. What I saw were examples of a very dysfunctional love.

My mother, who passed away in May of 2013, was the perfect example of love for others first. Loving and caring for others was her reason to be alive. When her body started to malfunction and it was time for someone else to care for her, she felt ashamed and she thought that being dead was a better option. She did not have any self-love. She allowed abuse, verbal and physical, both from my father and from herself, which is even worse. She was totally identified with her voice in the head. And her voice was not very nice at all. She didn't feel pretty. She did not feel she was smart, every negative self-judgment that you can imagine, her Limbo used against her.

In addition to her negative inner voice, on the outside she had my father to reinforce what she already thought of herself. And the lesson that she communicated to us was that of "love is a sacrifice," and I believed it.

On the other hand, there was the love that my dad was communicating: 'Love is about me, and only me. And when someone does not agree with me then violence is a perfectly good option.' Of course, neither of them loved themselves. Both abused their bodies with an extreme use of alcohol and cigarettes, for my dad. Negative thoughts for my mother. Both abused themselves through their thoughts. My mother would judge herself routinely then pray for her dead to her God. My dad would escape his mind through alcohol or the abuse of others. He carried so much anger towards his past, and he made sure the people in his present had a taste of that past he carried around.

As my Limbo was conditioned by these two extremes, I made a choice to be like my mother. Abuse and anger were not my personal choice, though I reacted similar to my father when certain triggers were pulled. From my mother, I took the self-esteem issues, the victim role. The "love is suffering" attitude and the "nobody loves me" character. From my dad, I took the extreme explosive jealousy attacks, possessiveness, and distrust. For years, I identified with these roles and believed that those characteristics were me, and changing them was not an option. I tried to work around my issues by attempting to tame my personality, but never about changing it. It never even crossed my mind that I could change it.

At the age of twenty one I moved from my hometown in Mexico, to the United States. I would not agree with this statement then, but now I know I was trying to escape me. Yes the "me" formed around my parents, my brothers, my friends, my city, my beliefs, my thoughts and my traumas. I thought by moving to a place where I could start from zero, including the language, I could create a new Spirit Jordache. Of course, we all know that you cannot run from your inner issues, by changing your outer circumstances. I did it again when I escaped "me" from the Northwest to the Southwest areas.

However, I had no Spiritual Guide, so from age twenty one until my first battle against an Immune System Illness at age forty one, I guided myself at the level of thought and by slowly learning from experience, but never reaching into my inner self. Eventually, the Universe sent me the "Three Wise Men": a) illness, b) dogs, c) "Dani" and "Tina". All played a very important role of the discovery of my Self.

One of the first lessons I followed when I lacked self-love was expressing Gratitude. I started to express Gratitude as soon as I woke up, and just before closing my eyes at night. These simple words "Thank You Universe," set the stage for the entire day. Though challenges arouse sometimes, by being grateful for what I had and did not have, was enough to give me a peaceful day. While my gratitude was expressed for whatever happened to my life, I also tried to add passion to my doings. I noticed how my dogs would go on a walk full of passion. Tail erect, walking with purpose, proud and happy. Full of self-esteem and not a care in the world. They ate with passion, slept with passion and every day of life is just good, period. I noticed how their attention and concentration went 100% into each activity. Win or lose is not important to them. Opinions of others have no bearing into their happiness. Nothing is taken for granted. Nothing is ordinary.

The same walking path always has new treasures to be discovered. They are content if the walk lasts one hour or five minutes. I understood how dogs have this strange ability to make our lives fuller.

Some people actually study their behavior, but even they are ruled by Limbo. They seemed to have tamed the voice, especially when they are in the presence of a dog, or cat or horse, but it comes back when alone... So I chose to go at life in gratitude and in a playful passion. Like my dogs. Every now and then, my voice would try to take away my thunder, but as the years went on, I was able to just laugh at the Limbos attempt at controlling me. This was the beginning of self-love.

My dogs were not raised to be very social with other dogs. My fault, not theirs. Yet to them this was not a concern, nor did they hold a grudge about my poor attempt at being their parent. They know, by reading the energy of other dogs, when play is in order or a more dangerous situation is at hand. They trust their instincts and more often than not, they are right.

We have the additional capability that if instinct tells us something, we have the brain to analyze it. However, more often than not, the analysis is accompanied by the voice of the ego. As a result, we make the wrong decisions because we thought about it too much.

Dogs have absolutely no care about yours or my opinion. They love because their nature tells them to do so. It is not an act of love of humans first, but rather an act of self-love so pure where they follow their purpose in life. And one of these purposes is to protect the pack, and we are in it. Loving you pleases them whether you give them a treat or not, of course they will accept your treat also. They don't give a certain amount of love and then wait to see how much you give them before they give you more. No, they just give without reservation, condition or explanation. They trust their nature. Which is the same as our nature, Love. Only difference is that we judge, label, explain, condition, and portion our love, based on the amount of control that our Limbo has over us. They don't. Their sense of self-value is as equal from all other dogs. Size, color, gender does not play a role. Yes, if they were to fight, the more capable dog in a fight would win. But before the actual fight, none of them would feel less than the other. This would be another message from them. If you are to find the Love within, you have to have gratitude, passion, kindness, self-assurance, self-worth, and confidence.

Energy reading plays a big role in the life and survival of dogs. Since they cannot think and analyze a situation, they rely purely on their instinct, which basically is energy of different frequencies going through their bodies, and knowing by nature, what each of them means. If we were to go on a walk and encounter another dog, my dog immediately would go into reading the energy around, identify the changes. Second identify smells. These two clues will tell them, better than we ever could, if the situation is tense, dangerous or happy. However, we as humans could make the situation better or worse by our reaction to the situation. For example, if we as dog owners would give out the smell of fear, a fear energy. Even if the other dog and dog owner are not a threat, now both dogs have sensed my smell and felt my energy, and I would have contributed into making the situation confusing at best, dangerous at worse. Animals are so in tune with energy, whether it is loving or aggressive, we don't stop to realize we are the ones that could contribute substantially into the making of a nervous dog. In nature, all dogs would be in the same frequency, but by living with us, we have contributed to their confusion.

By the same token, sometimes owners are the opposite. They trust all situations, are naive, or totally immerse in their thoughts that they fail to read the danger in a situation. In these instances, the dog is confused also, because he gives you alarm signals, and all you want is for him to shut up. We humans by having the capability of thinking, we also use it to attempt to mask how we feel, while underneath the lies we tell ourselves, are the "real" energy projecting outward, which the dog always knows.

There are some humans that are very good at reading energy, which is a trait that humans have generally lost. They have replaced it with using the mind. If you were to Let Your Dog Out, you would become more attuned with reading energy. However, this can only be accomplished by remaining in the Now, and by getting out of your head, which normally is in the past or in the future.

My dog, or any dog, has never cared if they win or lose in a race or any other contest. They will be just as happy about it either way, but they will always give their best. This is another loving message, that you can implement in your daily life, you can do your best and detach from any outcome. The universe sends their message through our dogs, to show us that what matters is not how you do it, but that you give your best.

If you look at animals, when they sense a situation and the energy surrounding the situation, they also add a message through their body. Whether they are showing love, happiness, or anger, they add a body clue. We humans, try to con people by sending body clues different than what we really feel. With an animal, you get honesty. I will show you how I feel, and it will always come in an equal match to my energy. We use our "intelligence" to hide the real self.

So whenever you have an emotion running through your body, be honest with what it is. Again, the only way to become honest with that feeling is if you remain in the present. Otherwise, your mind, your Limbo will refer to the past or the options of the future and act accordingly, though you might not feel that way.

Presence is very important when any emotion goes through your body. Allow the emotion to go through your body. Do not make a story about your emotion, give it space to allow the emotion to pass through your body, and then move on. In other words, be like water, adapt, mold, be flexible, trust your nature.

Have you ever seen little dogs trying to jump up on the couch? Yes, you can help them up, or you can watch them try and try. They will either succeed or not. Neither was a victory or a defeat. It was just an act. No other dog will make fun of him if he fails; nor will he get a cheer for making it from another dog.

Humans will act differently, but the real message is from dogs to us: While they are trying to jump up on the couch, and fail, they do not walk away feeling "maybe someday." It just is what it is. While they are trying, it is always "Now." There is no goal setting, it is Now. What you think is totally unimportant. Life goes on whether they make it or not.

Dogs always have "enough." There is no desire into wanting to get a better collar or a better bed than the neighbor's dog. Possessions and luxury make no difference in the amount of love they give you.

There is no feeling of "wish." Humans are always wishing. Wishing for a better life, a better car, a better job, a better partner, a better self - wishing, wishing, and wishing. All that wishing says is that you are dissatisfied with what you have, it is not enough, and along with the wishing are the feelings of frustration, deserving or even the feeling of "I wish, but I do not deserve."

When you wish, you are outside yourself. Gratitude cannot be expressed when wishing is going through your body. I am not saying that you should not buy a nicer car. After all, my dog will take steak over dog food if you give him a choice. But the difference between our dogs and humans is that they are not attached to the "steak." If tomorrow brings scraps that they have to eat, they will accept it and happily and eagerly eat the scraps.

Could you? The answer is no, why? Because of: Attachment. Let go of it. Whether it is a possession, person, feeling, situation, or event. All physical things have a beginning and an end. When IT ends, detach from it. Move on. Humans show so little love for themselves that they even wish they looked different. A Pekingese does not wish to be Dalmatian, nor does my dog wish to be a cat. It is what it is. Whenever you wish "anything," love and gratitude are being blocked by your Limbo.

Dogs do not care one bit about your diplomas on the wall, nor about the size of your check or the title in front of your name. Why should you? If you feel that those things make you better or that you finally "made it" in the world, then your Limbo has total control over you. Dogs will measure you by the love and kindness that you give them. It is a very simple lesson.

However, humans place so much importance on their titles, their fame, or their importance. We treat famous or powerful people way different than we would treat the janitor at work, or even a co-worker. After I became ill, about 10 years ago, I detached from much of this flaw. Back then I was a Robbery Detective on my way to Homicide. I resigned because of stress and my illness and went back in uniform to the Airport Bureau. I just did not care what the title in front of my business card said. So many people thought that I was ruining my career, that I was a loser. Sorry, but my job does not dictate how important I am in the Universe!

Dogs will give you companionship, whether you are having a good or a bad day. They don't try to fix your problem but rather just lend a paw and an ear so you can feel loved. Of course, we already know that you don't feel love, you ARE love. Nevertheless, if you "feel" the need for companionship, or you are feeling lonely or sad, that means again, that you are under the control of the voice inside your head, your Limbo. At such times our dogs are there to keep us company and allow us to be as miserable as we want to be, without being judged. However, the message is deeper than that. Just the fact that the dog is there without any judgment about your feelings, and is there with unconditional love, should be enough to wake us up from the fog created by the Limbo.

We should be able to see that life goes on, regardless of our feelings, and if we remain present, as our dogs are, all the sadness, loneliness and depression dissipates. We "are" not alone, lonely or depressed; but rather we only "feel" those things and anything we feel we can change by staying in the Now. Love is what we "are," this not a feeling. It is our essence. We cannot be separated from what we are, but we can always change what we feel or what we think, as long as we become the witness to those feelings or our thoughts. Our dogs do not have to become a witness to their thoughts, because they have no thoughts. However, they do have what I call "fast-feelings". Those feelings pass right through their body and dissipate quickly, because there is no mental filter to go through. So if they are angry at my other dog, for being too close to their personal space, or wanting to take their bone, they get "fast-anger". This anger is expressed and gone sometimes in less than a second. They don't linger in the situation or hold grudges. Puff!!! Gone! This is one of the many instances that our mind is our enemy and not an incredible tool for creation. Let Your Dog Out.

Ask yourself this question, can you sit alone and enjoy your company? Our dogs can.... always. Can you? Dogs never adopt you as their owner and immediately after this new relationship is established, wish that you could change the way you are just to suit their image of a perfect owner. Of course, they don't, because they never wish. On the other hand, we enter a love-relationship and as soon as the first challenge arises, we want to change our love to one that suits our needs. In exchange, your lover also tries to change you to suit her or his needs. Relationship counselors then tell you that you have to compromise and make certain changes, and so does your spouse. Consequently, in order to make a relationship "work," you change what you feel is fair about the relationship, even if that particular change has nothing to do with who you really are.

Twenty years later, the couple might still be together, and both feel miserable because they were forced to change the essence of whom they really were. Alternatively, if you are LUCKY, the relationship ends, and hopefully you move on to better pasture.

Unfortunately, the most likely scenario is that you went into another relationship where other or similar changes were asked and the vicious circle repeats, on and on, and on. If we were to respect our relationships the same way that we respect our relationships with our dogs, another story altogether would come out of most unions among humans. If you have a stable dog owner with a good nature, balanced dog, the relationship is beautiful. The dog does not ask the person to become another dog, nor the human ask the dog to become another human, or a cat, or a parrot. Both respect each others nature, and boundaries. Nobody is changing anybody.

Can you truly give your loved one the freedom to be who they really are? Whatever that is? With whatever quirks they may have? Whatever passion they may be following? Whatever purpose they have in life? Live and let live. Any changes that should be made should be your personal ones, at your own pace and in your own time. Is this an impossible dream? A Utopia?

Well, you already do that with your dog. Why not with your spouse? Mutual respect and total acceptance is the key. Our dogs accept ALL about us, not some of us. Dogs show us all the time that the way they accept the moment brings them happiness and acceptance. It is not the particular content of the moment, whether it is a steak or a bone, a new ball or a stick, a shinny day or a rainy day. It's all in the journey. They are one with love at all times, so they are one with the moment, one with happiness. All is within and not without.

Do dogs have conflicts among each other? Yes. I have three dogs, and I have seen them get snappy with each other once in a while. Even so, they "roll with it." In other words, they don't hold grudges, resentments or feelings of revenge. They drop it. Nothing to forgive. Learning to forgive is a quality for the human that came along with the Limbo. So forgiveness is a mental process unique to us, yet the mechanics in order to achieve it are the same as my dogs: "Don't take it so damn seriously" "Move on." When you are in the Now there is nothing to forgive, because in order to forgive you have to project your mind into the past, to recall the incident and then choose to let go. Forgiveness is automatic for my dog because he is in the Now, not because he cannot think. Thinking has nothing to do with it. It takes moving on to the new form that the Now has adopted, there is no time to forgive that which is gone and in the past is truly gone.

Dogs don't see anything as a problem. They change it; they accept it, or they move on from it. Unless you are an owner who forces your dog to train or learn a new trick when they clearly have lost interest. You know that dogs are always doing what they want. Sometimes in obvious joy, sometimes in a surrendered state, or you just see them disengage from the situation.

We see situations that don't fit into our idea about the world as problems. People are problematic. My job gives me problems. My health sucks. My girlfriend is a bitch (not fair to female dogs). My boyfriend is an asshole or my money situation stinks. Everybody is a problem. If we could just make everybody fit my way, then I would be happy, we think. Your mind attaches the label of "problem" to something that simply is in the process of form.

Some challenges get to start a new cycle. Some others are at the end of the cycle. Nothing will ever fit "your" ideal world. Ever! We might as well make peace with this fact. Yes, some of the things around you can be changed, so change them with detachment. View those changeable things as challenges, not as problems. However, for the rest of the events around your life to which you have NO control (and trust me; must of the thing out there you have zero control over), let them be, become friends with them. As Mr. Tolle says, enjoy them, accept them or if the option of removing yourself from it exists, move on.

What am I talking about? Let's see. Do you have any control over your health? To a certain point yes; you eat correctly, sleep well, meditate, exercise, have no stress, no addictions, and get regular check ups. That is the extent of your control. But if the end of the cycle of life for your brain or heart comes to an end, there is nothing you can do. So accept that you can only do so much, enjoy the life form that you have and detach from the outcome.

The same goes for your job. If your boss changes the procedures and you do not like the new changes, you don't have to enjoy those changes but you can accept them or look for another job. This is not a problem. It is simply a challenge.

I can go on and on with examples of what humans see as problems, because humans are invariably dissatisfied with something. So therefore, there is constantly a problem for somebody somewhere. Our Limbo loves it when we have problems because it helps it have a sense of importance. "Me and my problems," "I have more problems than you!" Nevertheless, if you were to remain in the only time that exists, the Now, you will find that those "problems" are time controlled. Like the anxiety of the future problem you will have or the anger, depression, regret for the past "problem.

If all of a sudden, a knife-yielding attacker came out of nowhere and started stabbing you. Is that a problem? Is that personal? First of all, your mind would go into mandatory "Fight or Flight" mode. No thoughts would cross your brain. You would go into automatic, instinctive, training experience mode. This is not a problem. Your body would get into its "zone" and would deal with the challenge at its best capability. Same as our dogs would do, primal reaction.

I have been a Policeman for 24 years and my instinct, my training and my no-mind reaction has been my savior, time and time again. In my early years I would make it into a problem immediately after the situation was under control, by asking, "why?" "Why me?" "If I would have... "I should have..." "I wish that..." The problem is created by the Limbo. And while the problem was going on, the Limbo was very,

very quiet. Because your death would be its death too. The Limbo is not stupid; it is actually very clever. It loves that you feel that your thoughts are YOU. However, when annihilation of the body is a possibility, it will let you operate from your TRUE self. After, it fills your mind with thoughts so you know who is boss. At the end of the life threat, your Limbo would make you feel like a victim or a hero. Present danger is never a problem; it is a challenge of life. Problems are mind created.

Elite athletes, artists, dancers can channel their inner self to come out and take over and they then enter the "zone." The more repeatedly they enter the "No-Mind" state, the better at their trade they are. Because these events are not life threatening, it requires concentration, meditation and total immersion in the present moment to enter the "zone." Those same athletes or artists or dancers, sometimes have big Limbos. As soon as they exit the zone it comes back with a vengeance, to say, "You are the man!" "You are da bomb," "You are the best."

Other sports which require you to be in danger of dying, such as car racing, rock climbing, or even boxing, are easier for the participant to enter into the "zone" because they automatically shut down to avoid dying, however, it creates an addiction to the sport by those in it. Unbeknownst to them, they have become addicted to the "No-Mind'. This is the only time during their lives that they are not at the mercy of the voice inside their head.

My experience into the spiritual life was very slow. I had to basically "crawl," spiritually speaking. The biggest reason was that I could not let go of problems. In other words, it was difficult to stay in the present moment. I had to read many authors on positive thinking and imagination, as well as motivators, because my mind was not ready to accept the empty mind concept. I started to analyze my "problems" in a positive light, imagine positive results to my problems, and have a positive attitude towards my problems, but they were still "problems." I had problems. Therefore, I had worries, so I was stressed, even though I had positive thinking. It was the anxiety of not knowing how the problem would resolve, even though I was positive about it. See my dilemma? I was in a "positive vicious circle," but at least I smiled more often!

Eventually and naturally my inner being, my teachers, my dogs directed me towards what had been there all along. The Now! I had to conquer my mind. It was not enough for me to think positive. I had to be quiet and in peace. So regardless of where you are spiritually, do not despair. Your teachers will show up when you, the student, is ready. Not before, not after. You can't rush it, nor you can buy your way into Heaven. Stay steady, even if you see others reach enlightenment before you. This is not a race. It is a way of being.

Remember, I had to battle back from low self-esteem, depression, anxiety, and all the other symptoms that come along with them. Yet, I was not suicidal, never have been. So I guess I was not at the edge as Mr. Tolle was. I could live with "myself." I never asked, "Who is the self whom I can live with?" Not immediate detachment from the self for me. Take as many steps as you need, just keep on working. Never think for one second that you "can't" do this or that. Especially, if you are saying that you can't get out of depression or anxiety.

I am not a medical doctor, so you will have to decide what and how much medication you should take. I only ask you to not say, "I can't." As soon as your mind makes you believe that you can't, it will attack you with fear, insecurities, and "what if's." This will reinforce the belief, and it will get tougher and tougher to get out. Be nice to yourself: nurse yourself. Be Love.

Pay attention to the type of people you associate with during your dark days. Your vibration when it is at its lowest, is calling for similar vibrations. The Universe makes no judgment. It only matches vibrations, therefore, is very likely that the persons that you are associating with during these tough times meet your vibration. It is the same with the situations you are put in.

I am not saying to cut off all ties with the people in your life, just pay attention. Be aware; be alert. Do not allow your Limbo and your vibration to match you with reinforcing outside people, events or situations. If you are in a dark place and a person or a situation you refer to as someone "I can relate to," make sure you know why you relate. Yes, it is a lot of work, and it is up to you. Be selfish, and not as a negative quality. This is not a bad word.

My dogs care for the well-being of them FIRST. There is nothing wrong in that. Dogs love their pack, but they would not sacrifice themselves for another, unless the other is in a higher pecking order of the pack. Yes, those dogs that save their human pack member's life, it's because they see him or her in a higher rank of their pack, or simply out of love. There is no sacrifice going on here. They are not choosing you over them. They are choosing the Pack over the self. They will defend each other if they have to, against an outside attacker, but they will retreat also once their pack member is out of danger. Dogs will check on a pack member, including myself, if I am sad, yet they do not become sad as a way of solidarity. They try to bring you out of it through play and love. They know their well-being is love. They are love. I don't have to match my mood to yours or get sick too in order to care. Just care a little more for yourself. I know this goes against what my mother taught me, but I also know first hand that her unselfishness never brought her happiness. Guard your thoughts; observe them.

At the beginning of my journey, I judged my thoughts and changed them for a positive ones. If you must walk the long path, like I did, no worries. It is very important that you find your inner Love and reflect it upon yourself first. I spoke beautiful words to myself in front of the mirror, and still do once in a while. Read books, smell the rain, the flowers, the coffee. Enjoy waking up and falling sleep. Pay attention in all the little things. Express gratitude. Be kind, have patience. Especially with yourself. Be here. Now.

The past is gone.... repeat out loud: "THE PAST IS GONE."

Remember that no challenge has ever been solved by worrying about it. Remember the saying from an old man, "Most of the stuff I ever worried about, never even happened."

Let's keep talking about Love, baby! Everyone is fascinated with this topic. You can meet a perfect stranger at the airport and inevitably the conversation will turn to love or lack of. Spiritually, I refer to Love as the equal or synonymous with God, Universe, Spirit, Soul, Consciousness, Emptiness, Stillness, The End of Suffering, or The

No Self. So you have probably heard different teachers interchange these words. That is if you are referring to the word Love in its purest manifestation.

Nevertheless, that is not the love that humans want to talk about. Oh no! They prefer to talk about all the dysfunctional relationships they call love. That is the juicy subject. Juicy because our Limbos love to talk about the highs and the lows, the disasters, and the conquers. About the "bitches" and the dogs. About the perfect and the imperfect. And in this dysfunction, all of us have had both at some point or another.

Spiritually speaking, we all are one with Love; we are born in Love, from Love and out of Love. Spiritually speaking, there is another "love," that has nothing to do with the one we are. We are going to touch upon this subject because it is very useful to see that being a complete being has nothing to do with finding someone to complete you. You are enough. So many people, including myself when I was younger, believed that I would become complete and whole, when I found the love of my life. It is true and insane in a sense. Because it means that when you return home from the Love that you are, you will be whole and perfect. But somewhere along the line the message got twisted and misinterpreted. I see so many people obsessed with finding their other half, their partner for life. 'I will be happy when I get married to my best half.' I did it. My son went through it, and almost everyone I know wished for the same. Some, after many tries, gave up and now prefer to live alone, disappointed in love. Grouchy and bitter. They tell you they are happy alone, yet when you speak on the subject, "All women are bitches," they say. "All men are jerks" others say. You can almost hear a variation of the identical story from everyone you have a conversation with about relationships.

I can travel to Mexico or France, and you hear the same kind of story. It does not matter the language they speak, the culture they come from, the riches they amassed, the color of their skin, their sexual preference, the person's sex, or their social status. All have a similar story. They will tell you their particular detailed story, but we all have heard them, or watched them in the movies. The human race as a whole is looking for love in ALL the wrong places. You can encounter the one that is hurt, because their "true love" left them. The one that has moved into the anger or hate stage and dislikes all potential partners; the happy in the clouds one who just got into a wonderful relationship with 'the one," or the content one who just goes with the flow with their present partner because it is better than being alone or because there is no "one" out here. You probably have fallen into at least in one of those categories, if not all. I did for sure.

At the same time, regardless of what stage you are in, it is the favorite topic to talk about by most people. Except the ones that "don't want to talk about it" kind of people, but for sure they are not happy either. Did you find your "one"? How is your love relationship? What is happening in your love life? Tell me more! These are some of the questions that even perfect strangers ask. The main reason is because this so called "love" is controlled by the Limbo, and the Limbo is addicted to drama, and personal relationships always have drama. For so many years, I was caught up in the same circle, 'the lonely stage longing to have someone', 'the courting stage' "perhaps she is the one," if she said yes, then 'the brand new relationship in the clouds stage'. The monotony of the 'not so new stage', perhaps 'the cheating stage', or 'the splitting up stage', 'the hate all stages' and back to 'the lonely stage'. If she said no, the, 'what is wrong with me stage', 'the angry stage' and back to 'the lonely stage'. Something like that, right? During all those years, I was invariably full of distrust towards my partner at the moment. I constantly had someone to blame for the difficulties. I was suspicious of all, and there was always some sort of dramatic, possessive story running in my head, which most of the time was created by my sick imagination.

There was no "good girl" out there for me, but I was lonely when I was not in a relationship. I had my guard up against every man who looked at my girlfriend, and imagined how she would cheat on me. I was full of insecurities about my looks, my possessions, my charisma or lack of. Honestly, I don't know how anyone put up with my shenanigans. Well I actually, do know why, but at the time I thought God was trying to punish me. I could not see why being possessive was wrong at all. Why do you have to wear this short dress?, why are you looking at him?, did I see you smile?, where are you going?, with whom?, let me see your phone. Sick stuff. The voice inside my head had complete control over me. And it would tell me you are absolutely right in doing this or saying that. I was in a stage of trying to control everything and everyone close to me. The closer I was, the more I had to control the when's, the who's, the what's, the how's and the where's.

This expression of so-called love was never really Love. All those women who went through my past were the perfect match for my dysfunction. Our energies matched, and our dramas fed from each other. I was given, by the Universe, the opportunity to learn something I had to change, yet instead of learning, I walked away bitter, distrustful, and full of rancor. One bad relationship fed the following dreadful relationship. One lonely night fed the next one. I was in a sick circle, yet I thought someday I would find the one. Even so, all the "ones" that would ever show up would be the ones just as sick as me. I was unwell and without masters to teach me. Even into my late 30's and early 40's with my first dogs around the house, I would take my own time before I saw the primary lesson. And my bad illness, to which I had to take heavy steroids and chemotherapy pills, didn't teach me much.

However, eventually, a tiny light went on. I observed the very basic love I had for my dogs. How could I be so abusive, distrustful, dramatic, possessive and jealous and with my dogs have a complete sane relationship? I was to the bottom of sick, except physical abusers, but short of that I needed some serious help. From all the masters whom I would later follow, "Zorro" and "Morris" had already set the foundation. Pure Love was there in front of me.

In this case, my initial investigation into my pure Love with my dogs and my sick love with my prior relationshis was to ask myself, why the difference? My Limbo's initial response was, "You are fine. That love is different because you don't have sex with your dogs." So my first response was sex is the reason. Though this is a true statement, I had to go deeper than that. After all the relationship with my dogs, was perfect. It could not be that human love was separated from another Love to other beings by sex. Really?

I was missing something. Something so good as my relationship with "Zorro", "Morris" and "Chubaka" that just felt right. There were no words to describe it. Nor did I want to. If you are an animal lover, I am sure you understand how I feel. I am talking about real animal lovers, not anyone that has an animal just to abuse it physically, or keep them in captivity. Animal lovers, not animal owners. All animal lovers connect because of our deep, pure Love for them. Which, in reality, is for us, but let's not get too far ahead of ourselves.

At first, being an animal lover did not change the way I acted within my relationship. However, the wheels started to move. I love myself a little more every day just by watching my dogs loving me and loving each other, but mostly by seeing how much they love themselves. I was still acting the same way, but the blindfold had been removed. By mirroring or trying to mirror my dog's actions, I found self-respect and self-love. Finally, in my head, I recognized how insane I was acting.

I should have communicated with Olivia. If I did, I did not try very hard, but probably I did not even truly tried. More and more questions about my behavior kept coming to me. I quietly celebrated my small victories, like the first time I was not mad or bothered by her wearing a short skirt. Or the first time it did not bother me that she went to out to coffee with the questionable friend. Little victories, thanks to the furry little guys at our home. Changes came; changes went. I regressed many times, but something was happening. "Zorro" is 12 years old! The rest are younger. 12 years to get to this moment.

My Limbo kept on fighting me for the longest time. Why aren't you mad? You probably do not care anymore! She is wrong, etc. But once a little victory happens in you, especially in your behavior, it means that is a real change. I did not know anything about the voice inside the head not being me, but regardless, I stopped being so jealous and possessive, and I was happy with me. The curse of my father could be broken.

Eventually, from "Zorro's" arrival to this day, Olivia and I broke up one more time. The final one around "Zorro's" sixth birthday. That breakup lasted for one year and a half. During our time being separated is when I did the most work on myself. Self talk, self-love, more observation of my dogs, and reading the mentioned authors.

By the time we got back together, I was very different. I loved me. So when we got back together, my changes were very extreme, and as I explained before, my relationship crumbled. My "unbelievable" changes were just a sign that "I did not love her" according to her. I did, but I loved me just the same. This time I chose me, and when an excuse was found,to break up, whether justified or not, I accepted the fact that she wanted to move on without me. What was the key to my changes? I am sure there was not just one. Changes are like peeling an onion. Layer upon layer of dysfunctional behavior. Or like a light filter upon filter, upon filter to the naked eye. In other words, it is like removing 100 sunglasses off of your face, each with a different tint, filter and purpose, until you find the naked eye. When you make a change, a filter is removed, or a layer, yet you still have many others to work on.

You might say that I made my changes from different angles. First, I did mirror work. I also talked nice and positive to myself. I analyzed every feeling that came into my body to see what it was trying to tell me. I stopped being hard on myself, and I was the first person I forgave. I learned or tried to go with the flow of the moment, as much as possible. I relaxed. I paid attention in how my dogs loved me, and tried to love her in a similar way, without conditions. I tried to let her be who she was, but at the same time I gave myself permission to be who I was, and not pretend. Eventually, something clicked inside me. Love had nothing to do with a specific behavior or condition. Love is always there if you really look. My dog's Love is for sure unconditional, and it and my behavior do not regulate how much we love each other. We just Love. Basically, be and let be. However, among humans is "be who I want you to be, and maybe I'll be who you want me to be".

Humans have rules of relationships, conditions, and some even say that you don't truly love if you are not a little jealous. Really? Seriously? Humans will tell you that since their dogs or cats don't speak AND there is no sex in the relationship, therefore, this Love cannot be compared to love among humans. I ask, why? I believe that pure Love, like the one we have for creatures and plants has to be the same for all beings, including humans.

I would encourage you to write down the symptoms and behaviors that your Limbo controls. Make a list. Find the opposite of that behavior, be it jealousy, distrust, etc., write the behavior that your pet would do. Assuming that you are a functional pet owner, you will see that your behavior is quite the opposite, yet you love your dog "to death." See how many of the things you jump for, against your spouse, you would normally ignore, accept or even smile about with your dog. Now look for the bottom line on the why. You will come to the conclusion that you just let your dog or your cat be exactly who they are. Well, why not let your partner be who they are? Why would you want to regulate, judge and chastise their behavior? Who are you to tell anyone who or what he or she is supposed to be? They are who they are. You are who you are, accept it or move on. Yes, it is that simple.

You don't know better than anyone else. You don't live in their head, and they have their own filters in how they see life. Their filters are their own, and only they can change or remove any of them when they want or when they are ready, not when you are. In order to experience spiritual Love for someone, you have to start with yourself. You have to Love yourself unconditionally and totally. No self-judging and no self-critiquing. All animals, except humans, ensure their self-survival before they move into loving someone else. We can argue this topic forever, since there are acts of Love, where a dog has saved the human they live with, and it cost them their lives. You have to understand that the dog is not only protecting the human but themselves also. Their instinct is to protect the pack. I believe that if humans did not have a voice in the head, plus the conditioning from society and religion, we would operate the same way.

However, our conditioning since childhood has been to love others more than we love ourselves. Humans provide for the sick and the young, even at the expense of their survival. I am not going to get into a philosophical argument into the merits of this subject. However, all animals will show compassion and Love for those groups also, but AFTER their survival is assured. Right or wrong, is not the issue. But we do it different. Some people might say that is what makes us humans, well maybe so. But I can tell you that my own mother lived her life to serve others and put everyone else in front of her, and she died unhappy and dissatisfied with life in general. If we observe young children before they are trained into listening to the Limbo, you will notice that they put themselves first as an act out of instinct, we then, retrain them and teach them to "share." Sharing is not necessarily wrong. The point is that is a learned trait.

Going back to the subject of Love, there is absolutely nothing wrong with being selfish about your Love. By selfish, I mean that you ensure that your Love for yourself is never questioned or changed. Especially if you adore yourself, in the healthy sense of the word. From the stance of real self-love, spiritual love for you, this can flourish into actual Love for others. But the Limbo loves it when you have insecurities, because those will transfer into your love for others. That is why having a healthy Love for you is the starting point. You will give and get, exactly what you are.

Spiritual Love does not have to be learned. You can see the pure Love that a newborn pup has for its mother and vice versa; there is no teaching there. Same among humans, mothers Love their babies "to death" even before they see them, given a person without a heavy Limbo. Humans then teach their babies and sometimes their pets, who to love and why. And 'the' why, will be dictated by how dysfunctional their Limbo is. By the time we grow, we would have encountered hundreds of "love-teachers" along the way. Friends, family, television, or media. All will try to tell you who to love, how to love, who to hate and why. A lot of them will contradict each other, leaving you to decide on the version of love that you are going to give and teach. If you are lucky, and never tried to teach your dogs to regulate their love, you will find that they are the only real teachers of Love.

At this point, in your life, assuming you are not enlightened yet, you probably gravitate towards the people that agree the most with your version of love. The ones that love very differently than you, you probably judge and criticize, or at least you will stay away from them. They, in return, feel the same about you. Then add a pinch of religion to it, plus some racism, and now you get extremist love. The so popular syndrome of "I am right. You are wrong."

At the level of your partner relationship, you might end up with someone whose rules are either "too loose" or "too tight" or "too stupid." Of course that is your personal perspective, they are not right, but nor are they wrong; they are just operating from all the filters they still own. After many failed relationships, some people go to a therapist. If they are lucky, they will find a therapist who is spiritually inclined. Most likely, it will be another human that went to school to learn about behavior from other humans, so he will give you his professional opinion. He or she will "fix" you according to their studies and their personal beliefs. These beliefs may or may not go against your "gut feeling," but if it does, now you have a new filter, and this one is a professional one. Others don't go for trained help, but they seek validation from their close friends. Their friends, in turn, will give their opinion on how love should be, what rules it should have, who is right, who is wrong. You subsequently use this new filter in your relationship, because your friend "sounds so right."

The Universe will provide you with opportunities to validate your theories, because the Universe always sends you more of who and what you believe you are. This will validate your therapist or your friends, making it obvious to say, "If three people are correct, then my spouse is wrong." You say to yourself or to your partner "See, see I am right, a therapist says so, and my friends do too."

So now that you made your spouse's opinion or behavior the wrong one. Then you decide that you are going to 'help' them change, or make them change. On the other side, your partner has friends who validate his or her stand and you see how all this snowballs into more dysfunction and separateness. And this goes on and on, for years, the two sides of the couple get passed on to their children, who, of course grow to be confused.

My journey out of the darkness of Limbo went very much that way. Opinionated, judgmental, controlling, possessive, jealous and always right. As I started to get closer and closer to enlightenment, the rules and junk started to drop all on their own. Fewer and fewer rules started to apply with me, without even making a specific effort to change this or that. Just by the mere fact that I was getting closer to the heart, all those little things went out the waist side. I also started to laugh at my Limbo and fewer and fewer times I fell into the trap of believing it. Today, I cannot think of a single rule that applies to my wife and me, just as the relationship I have with my dogs. Today I am liberated, in peace. My Limbo cannot enter inside my head and give me a jealous thought. Or any of those negative inducing thoughts. Though the voice inside the head is mostly quiet, I cannot say that I don't think. However, when I do, it is not putting on a tantrum because life is not "my way." No more games in the head, no ego trips. The few times that my Limbo talks, is to wish my wife was in the same page as me, but then I remind myself that it is what it is, and it is perfect. I know I am on my path, and she is in hers. Everyone has their own speed, and some may only get there at the time of the death of the body and it's OK. All I can do is to be myself and detach from any outcome. I Let My Dog Out!

Lao Tzu had it right when he said, "The more rules you make the more rule-breakers you create." Sometimes it is not because you really want to break a rule, sometimes you just want to be you and forget the rules. Sometimes there are too many rules to remember, or the rules contradict your beliefs, or worse, they contradict your instinct. Sometimes you know deep inside that your partner is setting a rule that goes very much against what you feel is right. That is a big reason to have few or no rules for your relationship, or they will let you down for sure.

In any relationship, you should feel free to be whoever you are. Even if it sounds crazy, but the problem starts right away when we don't communicate exactly whom we are. I have spoken to couples that have stayed together for a long time, and I have come to the conclusion that most of them stayed together for the wrong reason. Some of them seemed to get it right; they allow their partner to be free and be whomever they want to be, there are no rules or very few. They allow each other to be whomever they want to be, and pursue whatever hobbies they want to pursue, and they encourage each other to be the best they can be, while at the same time remaining as best friends, yet independent.

Now, that is easier said than done when your Limbo gets in the way and tells you that whatever she, or he is doing is wrong. Allowing your partner to be an individual and express their inner feelings and desires always seems to make the relationship less dense. I know there is invariably the possibility that your partner loves drama and makes a mess of their freedom, but that is a very worthy opportunity because you don't need drama in your life. Let them go if the freedom you allow them to have is too much. What else could they want?

And there is the other long lasting relationship that we all have come across, the one, like my mother, where one of the partners gives in to the abuse from the other, and feels that such sacrifice is the best for the family union. My mom stayed within my dad's rules and even when she followed them, he abused her. He abused her physically, other times mentally and often just because drama was a necessity for his Limbo. Either way, she lost. What she could not understand is that, as long as she felt like a victim, the Universe would always deliver exactly those situations to reinforce her beliefs. Yes, my mom asked for it, whether I like it or not. She followed rules set by my father, but they were not at any time too much, because she was never enough to herself. Though she complained, my father's rules were OK with her, in an subconscious way.

Understand that the minute you are enough for yourself, the abuser will leave. Like magic. However, even if you are severely abused mentally or physically and you have broken "their" rules a little, that is your inner soul asking to survive. It is like a little message saying, "Wake up!" I saw it with my mother. I saw it in me. I saw it in my friend's stories. Your inner self wants to survive, and abuse kills it. I saw fewer rebellions coming out of my mother than from me, because I know she had more fear than me. Yet, I saw it.

I saw my mother stretch my dad's rules so she could breathe. She broke a rule once in a while, even if to you and me, it seemed like a minuscule rule. Like to go and have coffee with a girlfriend without his permission. Your world is what you believe it is, so when you see an abused life the logical question is, "Why doesn't he or she just get out? It is not that easy for them. Your voice inside the head is very different from another. Let them live with their voice until they are ready to let go. The control that the Limbo has over an abused person is much stronger than from a healthy seemingly normal one.

My father physically abused me, but I learned to overcome it by repeating positive mantras to myself over and over. That was sufficient for me, but for others, it seems much more complicated than that. Understand that if any of these people reach out for spiritual guidance, it is because they are ready, and it will be possible to take them to the Promised Land. However, if you try to reach out to someone who is not ready, it will be virtually impossible to help because they do not want help. If you are reading this book or any other spiritual book, and you are abused, that means that you can be guided. Even so, trying to tell someone that they "need" this or that book, most likely will result in a disagreement and a possible loss of friendship. People do not like to hear that they need this or that; the teachers will show when the student is ready, period.

Furthermore, you must understand that there is not one key to change. All spiritual paths lead to the same heaven, but there are many, many paths to follow. Your energy field will match automatically to the appropriate teacher and not the other way around. So even if your friends are telling you to follow their path, do not listen, for your path is yours and yours only. You must walk it alone, and at your own pace. Believe something to be authentic when your heart knows it to be true, and not before.

If you are in a similar path as mine, and your pets have been wonderful masters, then by all means keep going. On the other hand, if it is a different path you choose, so be it. In my case, I had to shed all my insecurities and negativity like you peel an onion, layer by layer, until there was "no-thing," the formless presence. I practiced different things at the same time I was doing mirror exercises. I was talking and thinking positive. I interrupted my own negative thoughts. I analyzed my feelings to try to understand why I felt this way or another. I observed my dogs and tried to stay in a quiet mind like them (they always won). I allowed the present moment to be as it always is and resisted the urge to fight it. I gave myself permission to be exactly who I am by observing what actions made me smile.

Eventually, it clicked. I submerged myself into Love. At first, I was trying to decide what and whom I loved, then avoid what I did not love. That was a lost battle, because all is Love. I let go of all rules about myself or about my relationships or life. I can't emphasize enough: "more rules you make, the more rule breakers you create." I see no rules among my dogs. They only react when they feel threatened or bothered, but then they immediately go back to their state of presence and peace.

I realized that the rules I placed upon myself were, in reality, rules that society had placed upon us, and our fear of not clicking with the rest, made us adopt them. The rules I had upon my relationship were out of my own fears and insecurities. When the Love within me grew, or when I finally found that I Am Love, all the rules automatically dropped, I did not have to make a conscious thought specifically directing me to drop this or that, they automatically left my inner self.

As the light of Love started to shine brighter and brighter within me, I released fears and insecurities, negativity and darkness. All those things that I had read about automatically became me. I walked like my dogs on a walk, proud, aware, happy, and present. My mind finally rested, there were very few useless thoughts, and for sure none were negative. I required less sleep, because I had more energy and clarity. I realized that I made life into a problem or as a challenge. I choose that it is challenging, yet very enjoyable. My sense of Love was my torch; automatically opposite energy people, events and situations were not in my radar. I finally understood how the power of all vibration works.

Of course, the more results I saw, the more excited I got. I am not going to lie to you and pretend that my Limbo doesn't come out at all, and that I am one hundred percent enlightened. No, but most of my time I am there, I pay attention to the circumstances that trigger my Limbo and work on it. Nowadays, my work is less difficult than when I started this journey. I simply stay in the present moment and allow whatever it is that I feel to pass through my body. I don't identify myself with whatever I am feeling, and I forgive myself, every time, for allowing the Limbo to get the best of me.

I finally understand why we Love our dogs so much, and they us. There was no time even in my darkest hours that I did not go back into the present moment while being and playing with them. So number **1** is Love, based in the present moment. I allowed them to be dogs, and me a **human**.

So number **2**, allow each other to be exactly who they are, who they really ARE. Make no particular rules upon them other than the basic ones for their own safety.

So, number **3**, live with no rules. We made each other feel the best, in whatever circumstance, when we relax and take it easy.

So number **4**, the only reality that exists is the Now. So enjoy it because that is all you have, and always is as it is.

My dogs never interrupted my activities because of a worry or a future event they had to reserve energy for, so **#5,** the future is uncertain so leave it there. The future may not come, so do all the crazy things you want to do, now. Worries are nonexistent. They are the product of our human Limbo and all they ever do is take away from the present moment.

My dogs, and I, for that matter, don't care how foolish we look or who is watching or what they are thinking, so number **6**, detach from all opinions and judgments from others and live your life as crazy as you want.

My old dog plays as hard as the young one, so **#7**, you are never too old to do anything. Only you can set your limitations. And trust me, there are no limitations.

When my dogs fail at something they quickly move to another way or simply move on, so **#8**; accept no failure just detach from outcome, and if you still can't do it, move on and don't look back.

My dogs love their toys but not the price or the designer of it, so **#9**; play with all the toys you have but do not concern yourself with the maker or the status it will give you. Just play and move on. My dogs lose their toys once in a while, they don't care; let go of your identification with your possessions, enjoy them, but if you lose them, do not allow your Limbo to make a problem for their loss. You are not your possessions.

Dogs die with dignity. Their instinct knows that is the end to the cycle of their body, nothing else, so **#10**; dying is not a problem, it's just a cycle ending, embrace it because you will then join the Universe and the corresponding energy.

Love, Heaven, Stillness, Nirvana, The End of Suffering, God, Presence, The Vortex, The Zone; whatever you want to call it. All is Within **you**, not outside you. Humans keep trying to get there through relationships with the outside world, yet they never go inside and tidy up their own temple. So the search goes on and on, and the frustration keeps mounting in their outer world. They accomplish this or that, or find this or that relationship, or get so many toys, awards, diplomas, or they obtain popularity and social status. They search for special situations and thrills. They read all the books and get the most knowledge. They work their body out to an extreme to obtain the best look possible, including surgery to be the best look possible. They want the famous friends and throw their connections out to give themselves a higher sense of self. And none of them will or ever give us eternal real peace and Love. Maybe the magazines fool you into this possibility, but they can't hide the how some of the famous die, on many occasions, such as overdose or suicide, or the drama that they go through. Why? Because they never go into their inner self and find it there, or sometimes it is too late. I am in no way telling you not to obtain all the things and possessions you ever wanted, and even more; go get them! enjoy them while they last. Then detach from outcome, because ALL outside things have a cycle and end, or die, including your body, therefore, NOTHING at all in the level of form lasts forever...NOTHING.

# CHAPTER 11

## To Be or Not To Be?

My complete transformation from "not -being" into being came after my relationship with Olivia finally crumbled. During the last few months of our relationship, I had already been reading quite a lot of spiritual material. I also changed a lot of my old habits. Specifically to our relationship, I had gained a lot of self-love. Just the fact I told myself in the mirror that I mattered, that I was beautiful, and that I loved the image of my reflection. My self-confidence and self- esteem skyrocketed.

With self-love, the emotions of jealousy and possessiveness turned off on their own. I never had to work on the big "J" again, or possessiveness. For me, it was an automatic switch. It was amazing after finding the Love within; it had taken away those habits. I am not sure if it would be the same for you, but I think I am into something. I would think that it would be worth practicing.

In any event, by not having the emotions of jealousy or possessiveness, I found those last few months with her were very peaceful. I could be me, and I did not have to worry about where she was or whom she was with. My mind did not have any room to create those horrible stories that your Limbo creates when you are being consumed by jealousy. I guess I should have explained myself to Olivia, because I suspect I was sending a very different message. While I was at peace, whether working in the garage, painting, gardening or reading, she was taking my lack of drama and control as a message that conveyed either lack of love for her, or as she told me, before we split up, that I was probably seeing someone else.

We were in very different energy fields. I can't say that I blame her. After all, we put each other through so much drama for nearly 13 years that very likely my change was too drastic and extreme. And I never tried to communicate my changes to her. I kept it to myself. In addition, having different energy fields, it was logical that our vibration would reject each other naturally. Our frequencies were uncomfortable with each other, and we could not work through it. I had no issue with her spending time with her friends, or would not drill her with questions about her whereabouts, nor I would call her every twenty minutes to find out where she was. The feeling of distrust, just did not come, but I guess that was suspicious. If I could give you some advice now, it is that if you are going through a spiritual transformation and your spouse or partner is not in the same page, at the very least communicate with them. Especially if your changes were as dramatic as mine were.

My high energy was giving me so much happiness and peacefulness. I had not even discovered the process of meditation yet, the Now or enlightenment. I was still at the level of mind, but positive thinking, and motivation, and those changes already occurred. If I had communicated with her, maybe we could have worked on lifting her energy too. Nevertheless, at this point, my energy was not matching well with hers. She did not welcome the changes as I imagined would happen. The lack of drama was not my "normal" self. Something was wrong. I guess if I were in her shoes I would have possibly reacted the same way. Eventually, an opportunity to tell me good-bye was put into her hands. It was such an unbelievable reason, that when she told me we were finished, I truly believed she was joking. However, this was not April's Fool's Day. She was ending it for real.

I did not cry, nor did I plead. I loved her but for the first time during my life, I loved myself, and I knew I would be OK. I also understood that you can't force anyone to be or do anything that they don't want to be or do. I accepted her decision. I am sure looking back, that this reaction was probably another very suspicious reaction on my part. No sadness, no anger, no shock, no depression entered into my body.

Humans have the wrong notion that if you don't hurt, then you don't love, but let me tell you that if you hurt when you love, it is not Love. I loved her enough to let her be free, to make her own decisions and to follow her heart. I had embraced the famous sutra of "It is what it is," and I lived by it. I did not argue her "good-bye," that was no longer my modus operandi. Of course, it was very unusual behavior for me, so her mind said I was no longer in love. Truth needs no defense, so this was her truth, even if the truth was very different.

Was I enlightened? No. As I explained I was just operating on positive thinking and self-love. The Limbo in my head was not quiet, but I had control over it. Suffering was not something that I was going to embrace easily, or as a way of life. My mind and my body, I forced them to go with the flow of life. I said forced, because it did not come naturally. I had to be very aware of my thoughts, sometimes interrupt them, or even tell myself to 'shut up!'. I could not quiet my mind, so at the very least it was going to say what I wanted. Yes, it was a constant battle. My Limbo was very sneaky and would try to come up with some sort of negative, judgmental or paranoiac comment, so I had to constantly be working in my awareness. It was very tiring. I would go to bed in peace but also very tired. My Limbo was competing with my orders. I know it sounds mad, but yes, we all carry this insanity. I was tired of being the guardian of my mental noise. There had to be more than motivation and positive thinking. I had tried to read Eckhart Tolle years before, I had tried to make sense of the Buddha teachings; and none of those teachings made sense, or resonated inside me. Even so, that was then; this was now. Seven or so years after I bought *The Power of Now*, and it put me to sleep, I picked it up again. By now, Mr. Tolle had released *A New Earth* also. This time my experience was totally different. There was no falling asleep; there was no boring line or something that did not click. The LIGHT CAME ON! I could not put either book down. Being in the present moment, being still and the use of meditation was my new practice. I will forever thank all the authors that use positive thinking and motivation, but my consciousness was ready to be here, now. I found a way of Letting my Dog Out!

You don't have to go into The Buddha, Osho, or Mr. Tolle teachings; however, if they are clicking with you now, it is simply because you are ready for these teachers. If they are not clicking, yet, do not despair. The teacher will show when the student is ready. In the meantime, you can remain at the level of thought; there is nothing wrong with it. Accept it and detach yourself from any goal, because setting a goal would put you into the future. It would take you away from this beautiful present moment. To Be or Not to Be? I was entering into being.

When our final split up came about, I had already planned a trip for the two of us to Cadiz, Spain. All of a sudden, I found myself with no one to go with. I had made a decision that I was not going to lose my money, since canceling was not an option. At some point, Olivia contacted me to say that she was willing to go with me. To this day, I never found out if she really meant it, or if it was just a way to ensure that I would not ask someone else to go. Nevertheless, as it always happens, the Universe has it's own way of deciding your plans regardless of what yours are. Eventually, I showed up at the "Sancti-Petri Resort" on my own. This vacation would change my life forever. I already knew that there are no coincidences in life. Nothing ever happens by accident. What I did not know was, what the reason was, so I let go, and I let The Universe speak for me. Just the way I was to meet my present wife "Lilou", could be thought of as a script for a movie.

Here I was, thousands of miles away from my home, alone but so into the moment and in peace. I dedicated my days in Spain to work out, read, and walk on the beach. I have no idea what force of nature took me to Spain alone, other than to be in peace and full of positive energy. I had just broken up with Olivia a few months back, yet I had accepted it full of surrender.

Everyday in Spain, I followed my instincts, rather than my mind. Though my mind, my Limbo had very little to say. I was living each day with my Dog Out, and "without a leash". I had zero expectations, attachments, and any outcome was of no concern to me. Just being here in this moment was enough for my bliss. The light came in. I was awakened. At least for the majority of my time, and the rest was spent into positive thoughts.

My battle with my mind finally took me there. I heard that you should expect a big fall in your life, preceded from your enlightenment. Even though, I had other falls that had put me in the path of Love and Spirituality, it was my break up that had taken me there. Being away from home, on another continent, in front of the ocean, alone, was an incredible enlightening experience. I had finally realized that no "problem" is a problem but merely a challenge. And even though it is a challenge, it is a tiny, tiny speck of dust in the vastness of the Earth and even smaller, if compared to the Universe. By being in another far part of the world, I could see how life went on with or without me. It went on, with my challenges or without them. I was just a tiny atom compared to the grandiosity of our world. I was so full of gratitude for my experience and my opportunity to be in this world but not of this world. I spent my first two days just going through the motions and the flow of life. With a smile on my face and warmth in my heart. I imagined myself in the body of one of my dogs, and how they would just go by instincts, and without knowledge or care for the clock. I respected the feelings I had. If I was hungry, I would eat, if I was tired, I slept, if I had energy, I would exercise or dance. My motto were "Be friendly," "Be Now," "Live the moment and accept whatever comes with it" and "It is what it is."

Voila! It worked. It really did. My vacation was perfect! Because nothing is more perfect than the only moment that really exists, the Now. On the third day of my vacation, I was just lying out by the pool, when I saw this beautiful tall blonde. She appeared to be alone, and her goal was to have the perfect tan. She moved her lounge chair every time the sun moved. It made me chuckle inside, and thought that it was great that, though very beautiful, she did not act as if she cared what anyone thought. I guess I received a message from the Universe to notice her. And again I didn't know why.

On the fourth day of my visit, as I was walking from the gym to my poolside bed, I overheard a woman say to her husband: "I love it when guys take care of themselves first before relaxing and partying."

I smiled to myself and went to my chair to read. A few minutes later, the woman's husband came next to me and struck up a conversation with me. His name was "Erwin", and he was from The Netherlands. He introduced me to his wife, "Saba" and they asked me to move my bed next to them so we could talk. They invited me for a drink, and we spoke about this or that for a few minutes. "Erwin" then said this to me: "You are very cool, and since you are alone, we happen to have a single girl in our group, and we would like to introduce you to her, whenever she comes down from her room." I accepted, without expectations or attachments.

A couple of hours later, I had met most of the people within this group, which was about 30 people, from different countries and distinct backgrounds. They were all very nice and pleasant. At one-point "Erwin" said, "Here she comes." I swear it was like a movie scene. Here was, none other than the sun-worshiper from the day before, the beautiful blonde, walking towards us. She was in high heels and in a bikini, very sure of herself, yet not stuck up in any sense. Right then and there I understood the message from the Universe! Yes, this is my story, and it gets better. "Lilou", that is her name, and I spoke for about 40 minutes, slowly because I don't speak French, and her English was very limited. Eventually, before she moved to a bed to worship the sun again, she invited me to a party with her group later that night. Unbeknownst to me, she was there "alone," but not completely. Let me explain, she was there as a part of a group that had been financed by a wealthy man. He had paid for their whole vacation, so he expected the group to stay to themselves. From one minute to the next, the whole group suddenly turned their back to me. All of them, though friendly, became a bit distant, so I thought that maybe I had offended someone. However, I was in my own world. I did not worry. I did not ask for an explanation, nor did I apologize. I went back to my book and said to myself, 'It is what it is.' The rest of the afternoon went on without any particular events. "Lilou" also seemed to look away from me, and I thought, "Oh well, C'est La Vie."

Later that night I ventured into the Hotel party and saw "Lilou". I asked her to dance, and she accepted for just one quick song. While dancing she told me that she had invited me to their private party without asking her friends first and she had to rescind the invitation, and that she was sorry. I said no worries; "I am here just to have fun". She then said that she was leaving to go to the other party, and we said good night. One of the members within the group, who I do not recall his name, came to me and said, "All I can say is I am sorry, unfortunately I can't explain any further. Just be sure that you did not do anything wrong at all," and he left.

Now this only made me smile, because I had not a care in the world. I thought that whatever was going on was outside my control, so I would just have my own fun. I went to my room and read some more and had a peaceful night.

The next night I was at the Hotel Discotheque when "Saba" came to me. She said, "I will be in trouble if the wrong person sees me talking to you, but you deserve an explanation." This is the story that she related: She said that most of the people within the group liked me instantly; however, when the girlfriend of the rich man, saw me talking to "Lilou", she called him. The man immediately told "Erwin" to stop being friendly with me, and ordered the rest with the group to stop talking to me. He did not want another guy in the group. And since he had paid for all their accommodations, they felt obligated to follow his "orders". She also added that she did not want something to happen to me, insinuating that the man could be trouble.

I was laughing inside myself. This story was out of a Hollywood script not my life. However, I had no worries. I did not know any of them too well, nor did I care what was going on with their lives. I said, "OK whatever" and went on to dance. When I went into the bar, and I was standing alone, I was approached by a male in his 50's. This was the man who had organized the group. He came to me and said, "Are you the guy that is alone?" I replied, "I don't know what guy you are looking for, but yes, I am alone". He then produced one of his cards, signed it on the back and said, "Party starts at 2 am, don't be late," and left.

Later, I would find out that "Erwin", stood up for me and told him that it was wrong to give orders, about who to talk to. That is why he invited me. It was his way of apologizing to his friends. I still could not care less what drama was going on, but yes, I did go to the party and I spent my evening with "Lilou". The next day I saw "Erwin", and he apologized, and told me that he was inviting me again to their subsequent party. Before the time of the party came, "Lilou" came into my room with the complicity of her friends who called her to give her the play by play of where the man was, or if he asked about her.

Were they having an affair? Well, "Lilou" told me that she was nothing to him, it was just that he was the promoter of the trip. I suspected that he was some sort of lover or something, but I did not care. This was one hell of a fun adventure. Later that night I showed up at the party. When the man saw me come in he said, "No, not tonight, yesterday was OK, but not tonight." I told him "OK, no problem, but "Erwin" invited me again". He said "wait a second". I saw him go talk to "Erwin" and ask him in English if it was true. "Erwin" said, "Yes, do you have a problem with that?" The man said 'NO," came to me and said, "Have fun, drinks are there," then left mumbling something in French referring to me as "Gitan." The only French word I knew.

Why do I know this word? Because I love the word "Gypsy" and I had tried to get my personalized plate for my car with that name. When I found out it was taken, I researched it in French, which is Gitan. And that was my personalized plate in America. Now, I don't know much about gypsies, or their history, but apparently to be called a "Gitan," is an insult in Europe because gypsies are seen as thieves, liars, cheats, and to be lower than anybody in society. This is what "Lilou" explained to me, as well as another European friend I have in United States who is from Romania. But that was my license plate on my car and the man had just tried to insult me with it; of course, I wasn't insulted. And I was drinking his alcohol and partying in his suite. I just smiled to myself. I placed that license plate name on my car, two years prior to my trip. Was the Universe telling me something? Did it have a plan for me? Of all the words that I could have been called, I was called the very word that I loved.

Now, I am here in this huge suite, socializing, and I don't know if I am going to see "Lilou" or not, so I just mingled around. About 30 minutes into my time at the party, "Saba" comes over and takes me to another room, and says, "Lilou" is coming through the back door to hang with you, but she is not supposed to see you or talk to you, so we will let you guys know if the man comes into this room, but he never does." This was such a James Bond story. I could not believe my eyes. Eventually, "Lilou" came in and after having a nice evening together, said "Can you come to Paris? I'll be happy to show you around, and I don't have to stay with the group and I can show you around" I immediately said yes, and rearranged my flights and extended my return trip to United States.

I was just going with the flow, and I was having all kinds of fun. "Lilou" helped me book my flight to Paris, but even on the last day, we had to tell everyone that I was going home, and she was going to Paris. She left, via chauffeur to take her flight back to Paris, from Sevilla, and I left later via shuttle and took my flight to Paris also, where "Lilou" was waiting for me. I spent three great days with her in Paris and there were no signs that the man was her boyfriend, so I have no idea why he was so possessive and jealous. "Lilou" latertold me that the man liked her, and because he had a girlfriend, he would not say anything else to her, and was contented with having her around on his big trips. Me, coming into the picture was not an ideal. Not sure what happened there, but it was a lot of fun.

That was five years ago, and now we are married and living in America. True story. Destiny had been knocking on my door and I answered the call. I went through the flow of the moment, and I turned to "Being", like water with the flow of the events. I did not judge the situation, nor did I label it, and I had so much fun, thanks to the non- attachment to any outcome.

I also realized that even far away moments, even the so-called "insignificant" ones, are very special and with a purpose. If I was to ask you to take something from this unbelievable story, it is that magic happens when you surrender. The Universe is always listening, and it will give you exactly what you ask for. Just be careful what it is that you ask for! The Universe moved two worlds, from two different countries, two different languages, and two different backgrounds; and showed me how we are all connected even if you don't believe that we are. The universe put us exactly at the right time and at the right place, and arranged all the situations to line up, so we could meet each other, and decide if we could make it work. And we did.

The one big difference with our Dogs is that we can decide our future and our destiny, by the energy, vibration and imagination that we give and have. That is the beauty of being human. Take advantage of the lessons given to you by your pets, about living by instinct in the now and in total surrender. Add to them, a dash of good energy and vibration, and sprinkle your life with imagination. Let it boil in detachment; then prepare yourself to have a magical, delicious, succulent life.

Our Dogs and cats are there to teach us how to remain in the moment perfectly, be Zen, and be Love. However, they don't have the capacity of thought and choice. Exercise these powers carefully and be ready to have a beautiful life filled with magical moments, because all moments are magic! I am not talking about using your energy to call for a Bentley in your garage, because all form eventually dies. However, if you want some of those possessions, go ahead and try them, but detach from them, so if they disappear you can continue in bliss.

I remember one of our vacations on a cruise where our payment was a free cruise, in exchange for doing a dancing show, courtesy of "Pepe" and "Claudia", the same couple that allowed me to stay in the couples resort in Spain years earlier, therefore meeting my wife. Thank you, guys! Of course, the cabin was beautiful, but we did not have much extra spending money, nevertheless we had a great time because we accepted our situation as it was. On the other hand, we met other people who had spent over 20,000 dollars on this seven-day trip, and their mind was still in their business back home, and the trip was like a fog because they could not stay in the here and now. Physically, they were here, but their Limbo had a hold of them, and their mind was somewhere else.

Other people in the cruise could not totally enjoy the trip, because no later than the second day into it, they were lamenting that it was almost done, and they could not wait for the next one. It would seem to a common person that they were having so much fun. But part of their mind was in the future, making it impossible to appreciate all the beauty around them, even if they were picturing the next awesome trip. Everything has a cycle. Vacations do too. They are here; then they leave. It just is as it is. Many people with so much more money and comfort told me that they were glad I was there just because I smiled so much, and it was so contagious. Go figure.

Refuse the dysfunctional Limbo to take control of you. If your body is one place and your mind in another, even if it is in the immediate past moment, or the anticipation of the immediate future moment, you are not here and now. In other words, you are not living life; life is living you. I know that my Dogs are always in the 'no-mind' state and in spirit, wherever they are. This presence avoids suffering, which usually comes because of the voice in the head (Limbo), which judges you, the situation, the event, the persons and the things. Nobody and nothing is safe from the judgment. This kind of living will always lead you to suffering, because eventually, something or someone (including yourself) will let you down, according to how you think things should be.

Are you one of those people? Are you afraid to live your dream? Do you even feel that you deserve it? Do you understand that the the journey towards your dream is more important than the achievement of it?

As I sit here reflecting on the journey that I took to my awakening, I marvel at all the changes that are possible for anyone who truly has the desire to make the transition from Limbo to Spirit, before the dying of our body. At my feet are "Lobo" and "Morris" taking a nap, or maybe in Meditation. At the far corner is "Trece", also sleeping. And in the living room "Orly", the cat, curled on the top of the bookshelf. There is nothing wrong in their world, but I can finally say that there is nothing wrong in mine neither. Peace surrounds me.

On the sound system, I have another meditative talk from Eckhart Tolle, taken from YouTube. Peace reigns, this moment is perfect, but so are all moments because the Now is as it supposed to be.

# CHAPTER 12

# I Learned

My almost 13 years with Olivia took me from total darkness, to my complete enlightenment. I went from being completely controlled by my Limbo, to being in the Now, for most of the time. Teachers from all walks of life appeared, almost magically, when I needed them. My worst suffering, was my best teacher, and for that, I thank the Universe. I learned many lessons, and at the same time, I was a teacher and a student at the same time. The Universe taught me that specific people are here for a season, for a reason or for a lifetime, and to detach from outcome and pay no attention to my desires. It is OK to go on with particular people in your life. But it is also OK if others move on, both through the death of the body, such as my parents and "Chubis"; or people that choose different paths.

During my spiritual journey, my mother made her transition from body to energy, during May of 2013. "Chubaka" joined my mother in 2014. I celebrated both. Their purpose on this earth, while in form, came to a conclusion. They are free from their prison, called body and my mother, from her biggest prison, the mind. She is no longer in Limbo, and I am so happy for her.

I learned to read religion and to get the spiritual message from it and separate the man-created interpretation for it. I can now go to any ceremony and appreciate the deep message that is always there, when the Limbo in the religion is removed. There are so many beautiful messages in Religion, hidden underneath the dogma.

I learned how to go from being a people pleaser and enabler, to being independent, yet one with the totality of the Universe. As my changes were more and more obvious, many people left my life. Others I had to let go of, including my old self. And yet others, were feeling uncomfortable around my energy, and stayed away. However, many others came to me, attracted to our similar vibration.

Is it lonely on the top? No. I am most of the time alone in my light, but never lonely because I love my company. I stopped being who other people wanted me to be and started being myself, whatever that may be. The ultimate fear, fear of death has no room in my peacefulness. I understand that all bodies, all form have a cycle and die. I am at peace with that, and though I did shed a few tears for my mother, my father, for "Chubaka" and for officers killed in the line of duty, I allowed myself to go through the emotion and to detach from it.

Today, I know that Love, Spirit and Consciousness never die because they are the Energy of the Universe. The rest of us, made of form, will dissolve eventually and while in this body, I will celebrate, dance, be in awe, and express gratitude for each moment that passes. I live fully, not because I have riches, but because I am in the Now. I can speak my mind because you should never be afraid to say what you mean and mean what you say. Others will judge me regardless of what I say, and what those judgments from others are, is none of my business.

I learned that all the time that I was inside my head and in my imagination was never a waste of time; for my life is what it is now because of it. Everything has led to this moment. I learned to love and appreciate little things, like "Morris'" head tilt when I talk to him, and he seems to be trying to understand what I am saying. The beauty of a sunset, the sound of the waves, or the coolness of the rain. I am blessed.

I learned that if I can climb a mountain, it is never about being idolized for it, but rather so I can see the world from a different perspective. I learned that in life everything changes. So love everything, but own nothing. Accept all perspectives for they are a reflection of anyone's singular journey in life.

I learned that if you are going to call me by a certain name and put me in a box, then call me a "Being," because I belong to the family of all beings in this Universe, whether they have hair, feathers, fins, leaves, scales, minerals or whatever else. I learned that I do not belong to a crowd, group, race, religion, sect, team, union, nation, belief, political association, or any such thing. We are ONE.

I learned that the peace and the love I found was always inside of me, masked by fear, by my Limbo. Nothing can disturb me, unless I let it. I learned that somebody else logic might not be mine, so I listen with the intent to understand, and not to criticize.

I learned to laugh, especially about myself, and not to take anything so damn seriously. I know that if I smile at the world, the Universe will smile back. After all, laughter is truly the best medicine and comfort.

This is a biggie. I learned to follow my "gut feeling," my instinct, my intuition, my soul, my spirit, my heart, rather than my mind, my Limbo, my thoughts, my reasoning or my logic.

I learned that the biggest riches are freedom, peace and love, and that no possession, situation, event or person can take me there. I take me there.

I learned that absolutely no one owes me anything, nor do I owe anyone anything. I give without expectation and then I let go.

I learned that my behavior did not follow my beliefs. My beliefs are mine, and mine to change as I please, and not to please someone else. The biggest lie I was living was that my Limbo, and I were one and the same.

I learned to stop the negative chatter and replace it by practicing gratitude for all I have and don't have. Even when ill, I can be grateful for being alive and for the opportunity for my body to regenerate.

I learned that although my inner state will dictate what manifests in my Future-Now in terms of positive or negative; I do not know exactly how, what, why, who or when it manifests. The Universe is in control over those aspects, and according to my energy and vibration. I give, that is what I will get, regardless of my wishes. It's all about the vibe, dude!

I learned that water is much more than just a vital liquid, but if you really observe it, it can be one of the best teachers of life. It can adapt to any form, but not become it. The tighter you try to grasp it the more it will escape from you. It goes with the flow, as long as is going downstream. It has the power to overcome every wall, by being patient and persistent. It can appear furious on the surface, yet under the surface is always calm. Be water.

I learned that the Law of Attraction does not listen to my words and wishes, but rather to whom I AM. It never is about what I say or do, it can read the true vibrations that are underneath my appearance or my voice. All-loving magnetic energy is dependent in how much I truly feel worth of Love and my level of presence.

I learned to love someone for who they are and not by who I want them to be. I don't want "Orly", my cat, to become one of my dogs or vice versa, but rather I want them to express their full character of being always and become the highest version of themselves. Same to all my human relationships.

I learned to Let My Dog Out at all times, and not worry about what others think or say about my inner dog. It is none of my business what ever their opinion is. Nothing is ever personal or about me, but rather about each person's own level of consciousness.

I learned that I create my peace because peace resides inside of me. It starts with me and ends with me, as long as I do my best.

I learned that if, at anytime, I want the best for my loved ones, and me, I have to wish it even more for my neighbor. Though I know that whatever I obtain or get, will never amount to who I Am or who I become.

I learned that if I take a trip, near or far, to find stillness, it is a worthless trip. Stillness travels with me wherever I go. I bring stillness in to my travels.

I learned that "Heaven" is not a goal, a place, a residence or a destination; but rather the love and stillness that I bring into each moment.

I learned that though I remain in the present moment, I continue learning, for I know nothing, I am nothing...I AM. And I learn one great lesson......Chill Out!!!!

# CHAPTER 13

# Who Am I?

Am I a teacher now? Yes. Am I a student? Yes. Just like my dogs taught me, I should not need to speak and give you knowledge in order to show you where the doors to enlightenment are. If I had my wish, I would love if you could hold this book near your heart and be still. My teachings have nothing to do with content or information. I don't give you steps, or procedures or techniques, nor do I want to. I will point where the doors to stillness are, but you will have to decide if and when and how you will walk through them. In other words, I am more like a shepherd. Nevertheless, you are my shepherd also. My dogs and cat never uttered a word; they led by example to show me how to get out of Limbo. Find your own emptiness and peacefulness. Do not believe anything I say. Live your own truth.

I am here and now, outside my Limbo, in a state of no-mind. I am here, silent, listening. I allow my words to come from a place deeper than thought. The Spirit of Let Your Dog Out, or even better, become a dog, and become a cat. You can become anything you want. That is an example of stillness. Maybe a horse, or a rose, or a mountain, or the river. Only use your knowledge and intelligence when necessary. Quiet the voice whenever it is useless, and most of the time it is useless, then you will die without dying.

We are all teachers and students at the same time. When you let go of concepts, explanations, expectations, judgments, opinions, and rather choose to be present; at that moment your soul resurfaces. It is a paradox to say that you never stop learning, yet everything you need is already within you. What, in reality, happens is that you become aware of your treasures.

Though I am in the Now, in terms of form, I started writing this book over ten years ago. Ten years ago, I allowed whatever words pour out of me, to just come out. An outside force and not my Limbo controlled my hand holding my pen. One day, they stopped. More suffering needed to express itself. More awareness was necessary. I detached. For several months, the file on my computer stayed closed. One day, it opened again. Pages started to come out. I had no need to think whether they made sense to someone or not. They made sense to me. I kind of relate the writing of this book to when "Morris" goes to the back yard to dig a hole and hide a bone. His instinct makes him do that. One day, maybe a month or even years later, an outside force guides him to uncover it. My book went the same way. I allowed the outside force to come guide me and decide when I would be ready to write again.

This book started simply as what "Zorro", "Morris", "Chubaka", "Trece" and "Lobo", were teaching me. However, slowly, it turned into a journey. I realized that the story wanted to come out at its own time and only when I was ready. So I allowed it. I surrendered. For the first 5 and a half years, it was all definitely at the level of thought, I suspect that is why the words stopped pouring. I stopped to think.

Thank you Anthony Robbins, Louise Hay, Dr. Wayne Dyer, Don Miguel Ruiz, Abraham Hicks, Robin Sharma, Osho, Deepak Chopra. They kept my sanity. They kept me going. They kept me positive. Though the words had stopped, and I had closed my attempts to write, I felt thankful that I could live a positive life. My inner transformation was moving its wheels. I did not rush my state of consciousness. I had no idea that there was more to come or if it would come, I guess by detaching from any results, my inner being eventually asked for more.

I had a bear ready to wake from hibernation, and it was ready to eat. My bear was in peace, yet it was restless. I told myself, (yes, I told myself, remember, I was still at the level of mind). "There has to be more." "More, what?" I had no clue. That is when my trip to Spain happened.

I knew it then. I finally saw the Light. In all my previous moments of darkness, it had been my positive mind and the observation of my dogs that kept me afloat. However, this time it was beyond mind. I was reading *The Power of Now*, and it not only made sense, it was the only truth I wanted to hear.

Here in the western world everything operates at the level of mind, they always tell you "think before acting," your parents train you to think things through. Your teachers ask you to think your answers carefully; society praises "big thinkers." Your job tells you that in order to advance you have to acquire more knowledge. Your relationships are based on "what you think about me, and me of you," culture says, "think before you speak" and "think twice" Think, think, think. The Western influence has expanded into parts of the East and globalization, united to the Western power, has changed the way East operates too.

No wonder it is so hard to quiet the mind. From the minute you can understand language at around three years old, you start your re-training. Me too. The first part of my spiritual journey was about "thinking right, thinking positive," but think. The very successful authors I followed played right into the Western way of being, "change your mind, change your life." Nothing wrong with it, for they gave me the tools to love myself, to be confident and be positive. I have no regrets in having to go through that transition. All those days of repeating to myself, while driving, positive incantations were very valuable. All those days of looking myself in the mirror, directly into my eyes and saying, "I love YOU," really gave me a great feeling. All those hours exercising my body while listening to one of those authors in my earphones, were not wasted hours. All those tapes that I listen to, before falling asleep gave me wonderful sleep. All those times remembering to change my posture and my speech, whenever I was feeling down, they did pick me up.

If you are at that stage, enjoy it, embrace it, and learn from it. You are exactly where you are supposed to be. Eventually, your soul will ask you, "What Else?" The pure teachers will come, whenever you are ready. Not before. I am sure that if you are at the level of 'positive mind' you are indeed a better person so do not regret it. Remember that even those silent messages that my dogs were giving me, I ended up interpreting as if they were talking. In reality, there was the deeper, silent, present moment they were showing me. That was the real lesson, yet I did learn something.

It is not about the teacher or the lesson. It is about the student and the lesson that you take. There is nothing wrong with walking around telling yourself that you are good, and that you love yourself. Walking around while in-love with yourself is not a bad deal, because your perspective upon the world will change to a more joyous and harmonious one. Yes, just because you feel love for yourself. Following positive thinking habits, versus the Limbo in the head, judging and critiquing everything is not a bad trait. We really are changing our world by changing our minds.

But eventually, you will realize that you are Love, and that you are Life. But in the meantime it is OK "to walk in love with life." The next stage will show when is ready.

I could change my world via those authors. I started thinking about what is important to me and to understand what the changes I was making meant to me. Yes, I did follow steps, techniques, rules, guides, in order to make sense of my transformation. I tried to align myself with the positive vibrations of the Law of Attraction. I did ask for material possessions, special events, and people. Some came; some didn't, depending on how hard I really tried. One of those people was my wife. Yes, I imagined her. So, do not feel less than someone that is on another path of his or her spiritual journey. There is no wrong path, only what you make of it. Don't allow anyone to tell you that this process is wrong or that one is not good, and his or her way is the way. For sure, they are not a teacher if they say that to you.

After growing up with so little self-love, I was able to speak to myself about loving me. I started my own love story in my head. Since I could not quiet my mind, then I used it to stop comparing myself to others, or feeling less than. I convinced myself not to care what others thought about me. I purposely thought about all that I was grateful for. I told myself to stop complaining. I was my own best friend and established a good relationship with myself. In other words, I was always adding good thoughts, and subtracting bad ones, depending on my story, my dream. But still it was MY dream. You have to make your own. Go on and make it.

I also realized that the people in my life were a reflection of my inner thoughts and feelings, which created my energy, which drew the same kind of energy towards me. I was still years away from learning to skip the thoughts and feelings altogether, and reflecting my inner energy onto the world. And as long as I could remain present, the end of suffering would come. Nevertheless, I was at least trying and at many levels, it was working. Though I knew that winning is not everything, I had to start thinking what it takes to be a winner. I knew that my choices had placed me exactly where I am today, so I could stop blaming past circumstances, events or people. I could choose whatever path I wanted to take.

Through my thoughts, I could understand that I could choose to analyze any situation, whether at work or in my private life, and decide on my own if the impact was substantial, or if the quality of my life was affected. From that point, I could decide what direction to take based on my analysis, knowing full well that I could not change anyone or any situation, but I could change my attitude towards it. I could finally figure out the problem (I no longer call them problems, but rather challenges), take responsibility if I had any, do something if something could be done, and from there I started to detach from outcome.

My first few teachers in books and audio, taught me how to "think right," and I needed it. If you are there, trust your path. For the first time in my life, I could smile, at least most of the time. I had chains around my Limbo and the old concept I had about life and me had changed for the better. By the fight that I put against my Limbo and its needs, I could know that peace was up to me. Finally, I was thinking in a healthy way. Even my health got better by thinking myself healthy.

When I started listening to Abraham Hicks, I learned to create my own conviction or system that would resonate with my soul. This system helped me for many years to live satisfied via positive thinking and positive energy. Yes, I was operating with my brain, and somewhere in the depths of me, a little "Dog" was trying to come out. During these five years or so, I knew my dogs operated in silent mind, and that I was operating by a thought. I could see that something else or more work had to be done. But at the same time, I also knew that my dogs were masters of the Now, but I also knew that they operated below thought. I wanted so badly to connect both dots. Be a dog and operate in consciousness.

My teachers at that time, without a particular thought, if any, started to be insufficient. I had this amazing excitement within, with no idea what to do. Looking back, I was so close yet so far. If I could only stay within the present, the mind would be quiet, but I thought there was some other system that I had to research. I guess you could say that my dog was barking at me, and I was ignoring it, or at least not knowing what the bark meant.

I urge any of my readers to go within and ask yourself, "Where are you in your journey?" If you still have to remain in your thoughts, then follow your teachers but never forget how your pets are operating in presence. If you have already gone beyond mind, and you are reading, you will realize that yours and my journey may or may not have similarities. Heaven is here and now, and I invite you to find it in you.

Just knowing that nothing happens by accident, including the fact that you are reading this book, or holding it even, means that your inner consciousness is knocking on your door. You resonate with good vibrations, with your source, with your God within, with the Universe.

Eventually, I came full circle, to our origin, to source. I went on the quest of combining the simplicity of our pet's presence and mastering stillness. To feel its use, and to use my mind only when necessary. The next four years, until now, the best I could describe it is that I have lived them in and out of enlightenment. I moved on from my old masters, the ones at the level of thought. I kept my dogs, my cat, since they operated already in perfection. I now started reaching out to Eckhart Tolle, The Buddha, Lao Tzu, Osho, Ram Dass.

I will forever be thankful to my previous teachers. My life was better than ever when I finally became a positive person.

Once I switched to my new masters, I realized that it was quite simple, yet at the same time intense. I say intense because it was hard to avoid the grasp of the Limbo. As I said before, I had made my Limbo into a "most of the time" positive one, yet I still had the voice in the head. It was hard at first to stay in the present moment. I could understand now that I had to remain in the Now, whatever I am doing at any giving moment, at any time in a relationship and at any time in life in general. Yet, my Limbo wanted to show me that it still existed, giving me its "five cents" as often as possible. I could see that my dogs had no difficulty staying in the Now and I also knew that those moments of staying in the Now, seconds at first, hours and days later on, were the answer to the end of suffering.

I also knew how peaceful and in the flow or "zone" I felt when in those moments. My Limbo was almost pleading not to forget it, so it tried and tried to sneak in, and many times it did succeed. But I learned to identify it and observe it, trying so hard to survive. I am not telling you in any way to change your masters, regardless on whom they are. Instead, let them appear when ever they may. Your journey is yours and yours alone, and it will never mirror mine, or Mr. Tolle's, or the Buddha's. We just want you to see and feel the different doorknobs and doors, that all lead into enlightenment.

Mastering of your Self comes in many shapes or forms. I heard of people becoming enlightened by watching a cat, or by embroidering, or by whatever other means that put them in a place of emptiness and stillness. At the same time, I caution not to rely on any action or form to take you there. Because all acts, and forms end. By all means use your "props" for now, but learn to get "there," anytime anywhere.

Many of my early masters, such as Ms. Hay, Mr. Dyer or Abraham, had recommended that we should go into Meditation as often as possible. And I did not do it. Why? Perhaps because I was satisfied with a positive mind. It is obvious to me that even the Masters of Positive Mind and Energy saw the need to empty their mind and get into what Abraham calls the "Vortex." Even their answers, which appeal so much to us westerners, because they remain at the level of thought, had to come from a deeper space, where words or thoughts are not necessary. Their teachings came from the Universe, from the

Source of life. However, my dogs are always in their "zone," and "in-Source". In my case I wanted to be there, so my switching of masters came about naturally. I did not ask at the thought level; for them, I asked through my energy. There I found real Heaven. No suffering, no worries, no fear.

I was at a quandary. My earlier teachers were asking me to meditate and clear my mind in order to have pure actions, pure reactions, and operate from soul. I also noticed how their teachings required a series of steps, methods, or a technique, which require the use of time and mind. These so called "methods" did work on me for a certain amount of time, but eventually my soul wanted LESS. Again, I went back to look into my dog's eyes, and of course they use no method. It had to be possible. But again, I emphasize that this will come naturally or not at all, either is fine. No question. Allow your spirit to speak to you and tell you when less is needed. Not fewer possessions but rather less mind. You are One with the Universe, and the Universe does not require methods, exercises, or techniques to remain present. But you have to 'Know" it, feel it deep inside, until you are ready. Not before. Until you walk through that door yourself, then you will awaken, but no one can fool the Universe.

If you could, then all the Yoga and Meditation students and corporations would have shifted the consciousness of the planet by now. But the consciousness will shift when it is truly ready to happen, not when you call yourself spiritual, or because it is the buzzword in America. It will happen when the underlined pure true self in reality shifts. It is not enough to call yourself spiritual. You have to Be. And how will you know, if you are or not? You will not, because if you "know" it, that is not it. You will not know it because you will have become a "walking Meditation;" there will not be time to identify yourself as "Spiritual," though you are. This is what to me is the end of suffering, living the Tao, identification with Source, the God within, Heaven, Being in the Vortex, In the Zone.

The amazing thing about being able to use your mind only when it is necessary to make plans, or calculate your taxes, or pay your mortgage, etc. is that as soon as you don't have any use for it, you switch it off and there will be no room for your Limbo to try to make your tax payments into a problem. Even when you use the mind, it will be used from a deeper place of peace. You remain constantly mindful of the present moment and always a friend of the Now. You go back into a "No-Mind" state once the situation at hand has been dealt with. The useless chatter will no longer be there. By being in this state, you will have put yourself at a par with the rest of the beings in this Earth, with the added tool of the thinking mind to be used for the creation of masterpieces. Your life itself will become a masterpiece.

All beings in the Universe have mastered being, and so will you. Look at your dogs, and see how they remain in the present moment, yet humans have a tendency to classify all other beings as inferior. Humans will even classify other humans as inferior to them, whether individually or collectively. This is the product of the identification with thoughts and material things. This separation ceases to exist the moment that you become awakened.

Some books will give you charts of the Earth's flora and fauna, and will put humans at the top of these charts, as if we were superior or rulers of this Earth. Other charts put the human as the center of the Universe. This message is one coming from Limbo, from ego. Humans, in general, perceive themselves better than all other beings by the mere fact that we think, even if they are under the control of their Limbo. It is almost as if they say, "Even if I suffer more than the rest of the beings, I am still their Master."

Until this world can see that all beings are One, where we all complement each other, all of us with our own functions, none more important than the other, we will continue to destroy the planet, abuse animals, and even destroy each other until there is no more Earth. However, your obligation is with yourself first, just like my dogs do. Once you find yourself in a position of mindfulness, or awakening, then you can, by the mere energy that you radiate, pass it on to your neighbor. But it all starts with you.

You will hit your head against a wall if you try to go out there to attempt the alignment, or enlightenment of all that cross your path. First, is not your job; your job is Your SELF. Second, people (teachers and students) will come to you at their own pace and some will never come.

Writing this book has nothing to do with trying to force its publication, or that I get good reviews, or that I make money. It is not this book's job to seek that you like it, or that you are entertained by it. Its job is just to be written, that is it. The rest will come or not, and I detach from any outcome. It will be here to do a specific job designed by the Universe, and then it will dissolve.

If you are reading or started reading it and put it down, and later picked it up, it only means that its energy matched or did not match with you. There is no judgment included on its success or lack of it. By success, I mean in the eyes of the critics and customers. To me, it is a success already, because it was written from a place of stillness and I have enjoyed the journey immensely.

This book in no way is trying to redirect you from your practices, or to disregard your religion, nor to follow a certain teacher. Its attempt is to show how a regular everyday person can become enlightened, and the process that I had to go through to get there. If during the reading of this material you find a door into the room for enlightenment, is my hope that you will open it and enter.

My dogs follow their "calling," their dharma. They have no need for any teacher or book. It is innate. But so have you. However, the Limbo has taken control, and all we do is to point the way back home. "Lobo" has always shown his alpha instinct, even though he is 15 pounds, at best. Being a dog, and being alpha is his calling, and he does not question those facts. He follows his dharma without hesitation. He has no desire to be a beta, or omega in the pack; nor does he want to be a horse instead, or dream about it. "Trece's" dharma was to be a female dog, omega and a mother. Again, she followed her path without hesitation. She never wished to be less shy or more confident. She was probably born as the runt in her pack and when she joined mine, she fell right into her place. When her body and her calling came to be a mother, she did it so well, without a book of instructions. Just as rightly, when her instinct told her that her role as a mother was over, she started to encourage her babies to be more independent. All came naturally. And if you observe all the beings in the Universe except humans, you will see that all of them accept their calling with dignity, acceptance and peace. There is no cursing at the creator for being small versus big, or alpha versus omega. There is no complaining about what color or shape they are, or even if they were born with a handicap. Feeling sorry for themselves does not exist.

While the rest of the Universe flows in perfect harmony following their dharma and its instincts, we, on the other hand, were pushed and conditioned into thinking everything through first. A "gut- feeling" has to be analyzed and broken down into pieces before deciding to follow it or not. People have been trained into believing that the voice in the head has to reassure you when an instinctive decision is right or wrong. It is as if you have to have your Limbo's permission for anything you do or say, and even for what you are. This causes a lot of suffering because many times, your Limbo goes against your heart and destroys beautiful dreams. Your mind is an attribute that all humans have. A tool that we should be able to use and drop at will. That's it. It is another survival skill that the Universe provided. It is not you. It is yours.

Somewhere along the line we stopped being heart-centered. Somewhere, sometime, humans believed that their thinking was them, therefore; they needed its permission to make any decision. See how ridiculous this sounds? It is as if you are two entities that cannot be separated. The one asking permission to operate and the one that decides. Along with the "decision maker" or Limbo, came the judge. This is the cruel, the angry, the negative, the hater, the impatient, the fearful, and all of those personalities that the Limbo acquires according to the situation. The Limbo decided that your true self did not exist. The heart was not to be followed, and Love was changed to a feeling that required Limbo traits, or it was not love. The Limbo also made us believe that it was not only YOU, but also without it, life could not continue. Many people are afraid to stop thinking, or claim that it is impossible to be in silence.

If you were the voice inside the head, you would have been born with it. Children have no Limbo. It is the parents who teach it to them, or society, friends and school. So some humans have a denser Limbo, while others have a light one, all depending on the re-programming they received. Bottom line: You Are Not The Voice In The Head! You are instead the observer of the voice. Be the Light.

# CHAPTER 14

## ABRACADABRA (Hebrew) "I Create what I Speak"

Even if you become a positive thinker and you attract mostly positive situations and events, all things, events, situations, possessions, persons eventually have an end. So at many points in your life, challenges will arise. Yes, at least you will not call them problems. Yet positive thinking will only get you so far, because positive thinking still finds you in a state of attachment to things.

When I was in my transition from a positive thinker to enlightenment, I noticed that before the awakening, my Limbo was very much alive. And though mostly positive, it still had negative comments about this or that and made judgments, yes mostly positive ones, but judgments nevertheless. I was still qualifying something as good; therefore, there was also the possibility of a bad one. In other words I was qualifying something as positive therefore, something out there had to be negative.

See, as long as you remain at the level of thought, the Ying cannot be separated from the Yang. Even if you try. For everything you qualify as beautiful, something else has to be ugly, so on and so forth. So eventually you have to move on from that state, because it is bound to let you down.

First of all, you are not your mind. You are much more than that. It is great that for several years I could finally look at myself in the mirror, but I still had suffering, because my mind could not stay in a positive thought all day, everyday, 24/7. So eventually, I would fall, not very hard, because I was positive, but nevertheless, I would. My dogs never fell. Yes, it is possible that sometimes they did not want to be left alone, but their state of no-mind would easily take over the next activity. I eventually wanted to be there because being positive was not enough anymore. I was there in positive thoughts for nearly 6 years. It carried me through my illness and breakup, with relatively ease. But I did notice that I would qualify myself as a sick person, or eventually "an in remission" person, or I still would judge what somebody did or failed to do.

I was definitely still judging, quantifying, and qualifying everything in sight. I would repeat to myself "everything has a reason" and "love yourself." Both very true statements but you have to BE those statements, not just feel them or repeat them. There are many, many authors that will get you through the steps for a positive mind, and your Limbo will accept it because at some point you will say of others, "How can they be so negative?" (Judgment)

As long as your Limbo feels superior or inferior to someone or something, it feels happy. I remember "comparing" illness and treatments with other friends, looking for the edge of the biggest survivor. All because my mind was still under the control of my ego. I also remember being bothered by the fact that someone did not give me my "rightful" place as a victim of illness, and would not show me pity.

Same with my relationship. I learned that one of the ways of getting out of depressive situation is to repeat it and tell it as often as you can, until you have no reaction to the story, or your reaction is minimal. So I would go out there and tell my sob story to all that would listen, and I would quantify whom my friends were by how well they listened, and how much they agreed with me.

You can replace my story with any story that you have had and the results are the same. The Limbo has the same structure regardless of your sex, race or culture, though the intensity and way of judging someone or something will depend on your filters. Your filters are the important stimuli to which you react and qualify, quantify, and judge the world. Even if you are a positive thinker, your thoughts will be filtered. For example, a good Sunday for some would be a day of Football, any football. However, for others their filter will be their team winning; that would make it a good Sunday. For someone as my wife, who does not like any sports on television, a good day would be a day lying out at the pool on a sunny day, but rain would change her filter and her idea of a good Sunday. The football person would not see a good Sunday through the rain vs. sunny day filter, because that has no bearing on his good Sunday.

Everyone has thousands of filters that their Limbo operates by. Some are extremely important; some are so-so important, and some are low importance but noticeable, in their mind anyway. If you don't have a filter that your Limbo qualifies, the situation will pass you by, unnoticed. For example, let's say that for you politics is of high importance and so is Election Day. I don't have such a filter and to me, politics have zero importance. You will see your day through the filter of Election Day and go on with your day but always with your ear open to who is the winner. Upon knowing the results, your day will be on a high or on a low.

Nevertheless, it will affect you somehow.

For me, on the other hand, my day will not be effected by who won or who lost, because frankly, I do not care. If at the end of the day we have a conversation, you will not believe that I don't care about the future of our community. I would have no response or if my Limbo is stronger, come back with a smart-ass comment about politicians. Absolutely all situations where the mind plays a role, first it goes through its filters. Some of these filters are learned from your parents, religion, teachers, friends, television, social media, etc., but whatever is true to you because of your filters is your "reality."

Imagine being a negative person. If the positive people filter everything, the negative people have even more filters. So as long as you remain at the level of thought, no matter how many filters you are able to remove, you will never remove all of them. If this is sufficient for you, by all means continue your journey. After all, I have seen many spiritual teachers that seem to be in a good place, even though I never met them, but it is clear by their seminars that they have many filters.

Even if you choose to stay at the level of positive thinking, you could still learn from your dogs or pets, just like I did before interpreting what they seemed to say with their lessons. But you should aim at trying to be a Dog; live life outside 'humanness" or at least outside the dysfunctional part of humans, the Limbo. I do not deny my human form, but rather, I embrace it, but I go at it as if I go into a dance, with the flow and with the rhythm of it.

I know my dogs see humans as a wonderful species who provide for them and scratch their ears; therefore, they see us as worthy of their love. They don't even waste any time judging or criticizing our Limbo; they just exercise compassion and acceptance, in hope that the lesson will rub off on us.

Unfortunately, I cannot communicate with my dogs or cat, and tell them that I have learned the lesson, that I will pass it on to those who will listen. I wish I could tell them I understand the basic premise that you cannot fight the circumstances of life, and all there is to do is to accept, change or leave any event. I know they practice acceptance more than any human would ever do. What is amazing is now I know that my energy goes through my pets bodies, and they "know" I am at peace. I know that through the magic of energy, they know that I am a more centered person. I am sure they feel that. They feel the dog outside my body while in their company.

Will your enlightenment happen as fast as we can say Abracadabra? As if by magic? Yes and no, both are correct and both will happen at their own time. And yes, as if in a magic trick, it can happen all of a sudden. Complete peace, joy and stillness could happen all of a sudden; no wait needed, and as if it was a magic trick. Trust me there is no trick, all you are doing is going back home. Be here now, is the door to enlightenment, but the magic trick takes longer when you refuse to use "that door".

One of the most important things to be, while in your journey within, is to be grateful, including with your challenges and hurdles. By being so, you learn to live and breathe the mantra of "It is what it is, and I accept it." Even if your Limbo is talking, make sure it is saying, "Thank you" as often and as clearly as possible. Feel it in the heart;

create the magic. One of the doors to the magic of being in heaven is called "Gratefulness."

Understand this clearly: "You are not your thoughts." The sooner you invest your faith in this belief, the sooner the observer will magically appear to watch your thoughts. In addition, though you are not your thoughts, you do see the world through the filters of your thoughts. The combination of your thoughts plus your belief that you are your thoughts will make your Limbo take control and make you act accordingly to its orders. Aim to dissolve all your filters.

You might say, just as my brother once told me, "I cannot stop thinking; It's impossible." Then I ask you to do a little exercise. Tell a friend to surprise you and suddenly ask you, "Did you hear that?" And really try to hear any faint sound, really try. Your mind stopped in order to try to capture the faint sound, didn't it? Even if for a few seconds, it was quiet. Did you start to dissolve or disappear? After all, you were quiet for a few seconds. No, you did not. In fact, you felt more alive while listening for the potential danger. This is a very simple exercise just to show you that you are not your thoughts, otherwise you would have started some sort of morphing.

This is very different than if you ask someone to hold his or her breath. Eventually, your body will make you gasp for some air. Because you are in fact your body and the consciousness within. You would have died if you, for some reason, could not get air. If you were your thoughts, you would have to experience a similar experience of panic, while operating in silence. In fact, it occurs quite the opposite. You find yourself at complete peace when you can quiet the mind. Magic!

Lessons will continue coming your way. Some of those lessons will be so obscured, that you might fail to see them until days, hours, minutes or moments later. But eventually, you will recognize your lessons in the Now, as it is happening. Total acceptance of the timing of the lesson and the acceptance of the recipient is of primal importance. The opinions of others shall be of no importance to you. Nor, what they say you should do. The lesson is yours and yours only. The magic trick has to be performed by you, in order to learn it. It is not enough to learn it through a text. Do your best, even when you don't feel at your best.

I have seen my dog, Morris wake up with a bad back, yet that doesn't impede him from giving his best. There is no complaining, no judging just being what they can. But again, they live their truth. The magic of their truth is different of one another. Their body and their consciousness level are different than the other, though all connected. What makes it a magic moment is that they are fully committed to their truths. The reactions from the rest of the pack, including myself is of little importance to them.

The filter that you use to see the world is never right or wrong. It just is. It only reflects what you are. See and study the reasons for each filter that you have, be it jealousy, distrust, laziness, racism, sexism, etc. Find your reason for having them, then ask yourself if that filter is based in Love. No? Then is time to learn a lesson.

As I sit here writing, I feel a few lovely eyes staring at me. Lobo and the gang tend to stare at me often, and I feel inner peace rushing through my body. And as I look into their peaceful eyes, I see "my" mirror. My peace is also obvious to them. I realize that neither they, nor I will ever be duplicated by the Universe. We are unique. We are special. We are important. We are magic.

I see "Lobo's" caramel eyes full of love, "Trece's" brown eyes full of wonder, and "Morris'" brown eyes full of respect and adoration. Even "Orly's" yellow eyes show me care and understanding. This moment makes me remember the hypnotizing eyes of "Chubaka", and the playful, mischievous eyes of "Zorro". I get it all. I soak in their eyes. I become them. Peace is here. It is so incredible how long they can hold their gaze into my eyes, and I can't help to wonder how they see me and how they experience life. I understand how our eyes express and say so much and how their eyes never lie. Always honest. Always in the now, always magicians of life.

Humans, on the other hand, tend to avoid looking into each other eyes. We look, but do not observe, and all because our eyes are here and now, but our mind is not. When you put both together, the magic happens, and you let your dog out.

My dogs have taught me to follow my instincts; after all, animals manage to stay alive much better than we could, under the same circumstances. I have now, finally discovered the magic of gut feelings. Each of us owns that gut feeling, different from one another. Even those people ruled by Limbo, have an instinct. However, they choose to have their Limbo tell them if it is a good idea or not, and proceed from that conclusion. Some are only partially controlled by the Limbo, and every now and then they do listen to their gut feeling, only to explain it later as an attribute of their thinking mind. Some of us listen to the gut feeling first and follow it most times. Remember that what you follow and what you don't is an individual journey, and never wrong. For if you were to follow the voice of the Limbo instead of your instinct, how could it be wrong? It is right just by the fact that it is happening.

As I said before, there is nothing happening that is wrong, only lessons. Follow your unique instinct, which is your truth of that moment. Regardless of outcome, learn to accept it and detach from the outcome. Magic will happen the more you learn to drop the Limbo. It is also possible that when you follow your instinct, that you may find yourself alone among a crowd of Limbo ruled minds. While our dogs embrace and respect each others individuality, humans are very uncomfortable with the magicians, the ones not following the flock, the so-called leader, the popular, the influential or the powerful. Neither of these popular people knows any of our answers. Some of them don't even know who we are, nor care what we are. And be careful not to judge them or analyze them. That is not your job, but instead just move on following your dharma. Through silence and stillness, you will discover the magic. Abracadabra.

Throughout all of this book, we touched, time and time again, on the importance of the basic premise of remaining in the present moment. No magic or the liberation of your inner dog will happen without this important basic rule. Remain here and now.

As we move into the last few paragraphs of my journey, I can only wish you magic, enlightenment, bliss, love and presence. Do not wait for a dream to happen to start your journey, or to feel happy. Rather, enjoy all your paths and happiness will follow. I have immensely enjoyed writing "my child", my book. The Universe will dictate where it goes from here.

Find the love of every moment, enjoy and see your pets in a different light. Let them teach you the beautiful world of the now. I wish you to learn to drop all roles and just be your own Dog. Learn to be your own essence and not the judgments of you upon yourself, nor the judgments of others upon you. I wish you to go deep within. I wish you learn to accept all that the Universe sends you. Lose interest on your future and your past.

I wish you pure meditation, and connection with your consciousness. I wish you to feel gratitude, kindness and acceptance of any moment that presents itself, regardless of the form that it takes. I wish you to put your Being well in front of any doing. Do not become a human doing, really discover the essence of your being, and from there you can address any situation.

I wish you to develop a dog-like quality of the reading of energy, and the use of it for loving purposes. I wish you to find a way to wag your tail, even in moments of pain and grief. I wish you "real" walks among your dog, so he can teach you the beauty of a simple life. I wish you to understand that, though you don't know how to roll over or sit when told, yet you are wise.

I wish you the capacity to live and let live. I wish you the capacity to be forgiving even to those that took your bone. I wish you gratitude for all the treats that you may or may not get. I wish you being humble, and not knowing it. I wish you the pleasure to be comfortable in your own fur, and peace to know that is OK not to be someone else. I wish you the capacity to learn our dog's lessons, and see them as a mirror to reflect upon, without clinging to anything or anybody.

May the rest of your eternal life be detached of Limbo, full of silence and a walking Meditation. In other words, I wish you to Let Your Dog Out! My friend, go find the Dog that lives within you. When you find it, open the door. Invite him to come out and play. Once the magic of Letting Your Dog Out grabs you, it won't let go. Once your Dog is out, it will not be chained again. Namaste. And LYDO !

To be continued.......